HOW TO SOUND INTELLIGENT IN JAPANESE
A VOCABULARY BUILDER

HOW TO SOUND INTELLIGENT IN JAPANESE

A Vocabulary Builder

Charles De Wolf

KODANSHA INTERNATIONAL
Tokyo • New York • London

Distributed in the United States by Kodansha America, Inc., 114
Fifth Avenue, New York, N.Y. 10011, and in the United Kingdom
and continental Europe by Kodansha Europe Ltd., 95 Aldwych,
London WC2B 4JF. Published by Kodansha International Ltd.,
17-14 Otowa 1-chome, Bunkyo-ku, Tokyo 112-8652, and
Kodansha America, Inc.

98 99 00 01 02   10 9 8 7 6 5 4

ISBN 4-7700-1747-2

Contents

Preface

"Je ne suis pas comme une dame de la cour de Versailles, qui disait: c'est bien dommage que l'aventure de la tour de Babel ait produit la confusion des langues; sans cela tout le monde aurait toujours parlé français."
(Voltaire, 1767)

"...Seeing that you speak Japanese, they will wag their heads and smile condescendingly, and admit to each other that you are really quite intelligent—much as we would do in the presence of a pig or an ape of somewhat unusual attainments."
(Basil Hall Chamberlain, 1904)

"The foreigner in Japan, so long as he is not thought to be a permanent immigrant, is treated very politely, but always as an outsider. If he speaks Japanese at all, no matter how badly, he is praised for this remarkable accomplishment, as though we were an idiot child who suddenly showed a streak of intelligence."
(Edwin O. Reischauer, 1977)

Linguistic chauvinism, like other human failings, comes in many varieties. Voltaire's apocryphal court lady assumes that the pre-Babelic language of mankind must have been French. Today she might just as well stand for the stereotypical English-speaker who believes that the entire world speaks—or ought to speak—*his* mother tongue.

In sharp contrast to such naive universalism is traditional Japanese exclusivity. The notion that it is somehow extraordinarily difficult and even "unnatural" for non-Japanese (or at least Occidentals) to speak *Nihongo* is one that many a seasoned reader will have already encountered.

Nevertheless, the implicit premise of this book—and indeed of the entire Power Japanese series—is that the linguistic status of the foreigner in Japan has changed and continues to change. This, of course, means ever more demanding standards. The day is past when extravagant praise can be expected for the mere ability to use Japanese in ordering *tonkatsu* or filling out forms. More and more intelligent aliens will be expected to prove themselves with well-informed and articulate comments on a broad range of subjects: from ideas and theories to business and economics.

*

As the subtitle suggests, *Sounding Intelligent in Japanese* is a vocabulary-building book. Each chapter typically begins with single Sino-Japanese lexical elements, combined to form words and compounds, some of which are then repeated in the illustrative sentences that follow. Unlike textbook dialogue drills, these are intended not for memorization but simply for reinforcement—and sometimes even for diversion: よく学び、よく遊べ *yoku manabi, yoku asobe*, as the saying goes.

Though technical linguistic terminology has been kept to a minimum, a few key concepts remain. *Sino-Japanese*, just mentioned, refers to words of Chinese origin that have been thoroughly assimilated into Japanese. The Sino-Japanese term for *Sino-Japanese*, for example, is 漢語 *kango*, lit. "Han language."

Less obvious are the subcategories *go* (呉) and *kan* (漢). These refer to the two major sets of Sino-Japanese readings, the second both more recent and generally more common. Note, for example, *gō* "karma" in Chapter 2 vs. *gyō* "business" in Chapter 7, both written 業.

*

Loyal partisans of rival romanizations may frown at the eclectic conventions followed in this book. For Sino-Japanese words in which [o:] is written as ⋯⋯う in hiragana, I have used *ō* rather than *ou*. Thus, 政党 "political party" becomes *seitō* rather than *seitou*. The principle of consistency might seem to dictate that I write 映画 "movie" as *ēga*, but here the spelling reflects Japanese conventions: *eiga*.

言う "say," written いう in hiragana but pronounced [yuu], is likewise romanized à la japonaise as *iu*. Chemical names that appear in Chapter 5, on the other hand, e.g., *baryūmu* and *maguneshūmu*, on the other hand, are rendered phonetically.

Hyphenation in the romanization is based on both morphological principles and the more practical consideration of appearance. The desire for absolute consistency thus yields to the requirement of readability.

Except where minimal pairs are already in the text or come immediately to mind, pitch accent distinctions have been ignored. The author trusts that his intelligent readers are also astute listeners.

Acknowledgements

Last-minute revisions of outdated examples remind me how long this book has been in the making. To Michael Brase, who first proposed the idea and patiently nurtured it with sound and intelligent advice, I am greatly indebted. Special thanks also go to Shigeyoshi Suzuki, likewise of Kodansha International, for many hours of astute and careful scrutiny of entries and illustrative sentences that were either structurally awkward or socially implausible. To Masako Nakamura, my star pupil, long-suffering teacher, and wise counsellor, who generously checked each and every chapter and offered invaluable advice, I can only express enormous gratitude. Responsibility for such errors that remain despite the heroic efforts of these three are, of course, my own.

Finally, for putting up with *kapuseru ni tojikomotta papa*, a heartfelt *arigatō* to my wife Keiko Suda and our four children.

まえがき

文化のいかんを問わず教養ある人に共通に見られるのは、自国語を自由に操れるという自負である。教育の大きな部分は、結局のところ複雑な言語学的記号の習得に充てられている。この結果、不幸なことに、自国語を十分解せない外国人を多少とも軽蔑の目で見る傾向が生まれる。言葉の壁を乗り越えようと努力した人ならよく経験することだが、自分には言われていることがちゃんとわかっていて、普通の大人の"難しい言葉"くらい使えるのだということを話し相手に分かってもらうには、かなりの努力を費やさなくてはならない。

日本語を学習している欧米人にありがちな失敗は、ある時点で語彙を増やすことを諦めてしまうことである。漢字の学習から得られる興奮は時とともに薄れ、熟語はどれも同じように見えるし聞こえるようになる。そういう人は、英語でもなく日本語でもない中途半端なジャパニーズに頼るようになる。「ロシアタンカーの重油流出についてどう思いますか」という代わりに、「ロシアタンカーは……石油……スピルした。どう思う?」というように。

この本は、わざと教養を全面に押し出したようなところがあると言ってよい。これは、「現実に即した会話」教本をめざしたものではない。実際振り返って考えてみると、私は半ば意識的に、教室で聞かれる日本文のパターンプラクティスを皮肉ってこれを書いたように思う。単語や語句や文の意味するところを一寸ばかり押し広げ、できることなら楽しい覚えやすいパターンにして読者に届けよう、というのが私の狙いであった。

英文には、英語圏の人にもそうでない人にも「心に残りやすい」ものを選んだつもりである。日本人にとって多少とも知っている語録が多いことだろうが、文脈の中で使えるように心掛けた。

最後にこの本は、国境を越えて知性に訴えることを意図したものである。言語や文化の違いが意識されることは時にあるけれども、明快な対話は、一言語、一文化の専売特許ではないし、努力すれば自分の考えを他国語で表現して他人と共有する技術を学ぶことは実際可能なのである。

Introduction

*Barbarus hic ego sum, quia non **intelligor** ulli.* (Here I am a
barbarian, for no one understands me.)
(Ovid, 43 B.C.–AD ?17)

*Sedulo curavi, humanas actiones non ridere, non lugere, neque
detestari, sed **intellegere**.* (I have endeavored not to ridicule,
bewail, or disdain human behavior, but to understand it.)
(Baruch Spinoza, 1632–77)

"An **intelligent** boy!" said Scrooge. "A remarkable boy!
Do you know whether they've sold the prize
turkey that was hanging up there?"
(Charles Dickens, 1812–70)

Ovid died in exile on the Black Sea. For foreigners in modern
Japan, the key to escaping the poet's linguistic fate is greater
intelligence.

As students of Latin will remember, *intelligent-* is the present participial stem of the verb *intellegere* "understand, become aware of" or, literally, "gather and choose from among."
The adjective comes into English relatively late, and its modern
meaning ("bright, clever, perspicacious") is still more recent.
The various translations found in Kenkyusha's *New English-
Japanese Dictionary* include: *rikai-ryoku no aru*, lit. "having
the power to discern, *risei-teki na* "rational," *richi-teki na*, lit.
"rational and knowledgeable," *mono-wakari no ii*, lit. "good at
understanding things," *sōmei na* "sagacious," *kashikoi* "wise,
clever, (having) a good head," *kenmei na* "wise," *ki no kiita* lit.
"nimble of wit," and *rikō na* lit "of agile mouth."

Here is an example of *rikai-ryoku* "intelligence" by itself.

1. 大学の入学試験は、理解力より記憶力を試すものだと批判され
ています。
Daigaku no nyūgaku-shiken wa, rikai-ryoku yori kioku-ryoku o tame-

11

su mono da to hihan sarete imasu.

University entrance examinations are being criticized for measuring the ability to memorize rather than true intelligence.

Risei-teki na is less likely to suggest a keen mind than the general power of reason. As a noun, *risei* is used as a philosophical term to translate Greek *nous*, German *Vernunft*.

2. 夕べカントの「純粋理性批判」を読み始めたところ興奮して眠れなくなりました。

Yūbe kanto no "junsui-risei–hihan" o yomihajimeta tokoro kōfun shite nemurenaku narimashita.

Last night I started reading Kant's *Critique of Pure Reason* and got so excited that I couldn't sleep.

Richi-teki smacks of intellectualism, and though intellectuals are reputedly intelligent, appearances can deceive.

3. あの人は理知的な顔をしているけど、実際には馬鹿だ。

Ano hito wa richi-teki na kao o shite iru kedo, jissai ni wa baka da.

He may have the look of an intellectual, but in fact he's a fool.

Mono-wakari no ii can suggest a worldly-wise understanding but is not necessarily related to intellectual or verbal dexterity.

4. 百合子さんのおとうさんはものわかりのいい人だから、彼女がノルウェー人と結婚するつもりだと聞いて、すぐその結婚に同意した。

Yukiko-san no otōsan wa mono-wakari no ii hito da kara, kanojo ga noruwē-jin to kekkon suru tsumori da to kiite, sugu sono kekkon ni dōi shita.

Being an understanding man, Yuriko's father immediately consented when she told him of her intention to marry a Norwegian.

Similarly, as the English gloss implies, *sōmei na* more likely evokes the fruit of long experience (or innate wisdom) than the power of raw intellect. Note that the more or less literal meaning is "with ears and eyes wide open."

5. イギリスの国王がすべて聡明な君主だとはいえません。

Igirisu no kokuō ga subete sōmei na kunshu da to wa iemasen.

It cannot be said that all of Britain's monarchs were wise rulers.

Kashikoi is one of only two expressions here that are of purely Japanese as opposed to Sino-Japanese origin. Though written with the Chinese character for "wise" (cf. *ken-* of *kenmei* "wise"), the term originally means "awesome, august" and is related to early Japanese animism and the imperial cult. In some contexts, it suggests less bookish brilliance than practical awareness.

6. 静枝さんは賢いからあのエッチな課長をあしらうくらい朝飯前でしょう。

Shizue-san wa kashikoi kara ano etchi na kachō o ashirau kurai asameshi-mae deshō.

I think Shizue is smart enough that handling her lecherous section chief should be a piece of cake.

The native Japanese expression *atama no yoi* is commonly heard in conversation. As a predicate, the form is often *atama ga ii*.

7. 兄の子供達は皆頭がいいけど勉強しない。

Ani no kodomo-tachi wa mina atama ga ii kedo benkyō shinai.

My elder brother's children are all clever, but they don't study.

賢明 *kenmei* (lit. sagacity + brightness) might seem to suggest the ideal combination of wisdom and acumen, and indeed *kenmei na hito* may be understood to be both wise and intelligent. Sometimes, particularly in Japan, wisdom embraces prudence.

8. 契約を更新させたいなら短気をおこさないでもっと賢明にやらないとだめだよ。

Keiyaku o kōshin sasetai nara tanki o okosanai de motto kenmei ni yaranai to dame da yo.

If you want your contract extended, you'd better guard your temper and act more prudently.

Ki no kiita consists of Sino-Japanese *ki* "spirit" and native Japanese … *no kiita* (lit. having been effective). The meaning ranges from "sensible" to "witty" and "chic":

9. 直美さんはいつも気の利いた冗談を言う。

Naomi-san wa itsumo ki no kiita jōdan o iu.

Naomi is always telling witty jokes.

10. なんて利口な坊やだ。

Nante rikō na bōya da.

An intelligent boy…!

exclaims Scrooge in Keijirō Okamoto's translation of the Dickens' classic. Yet though typically heard in the praise of small children (*orikō-san ne*), the expression can also have a decidedly derisive sense. To translate *How to Sound Intelligent in Japanese*, for example, as *Nihon-go de rikō ni kikoeru ni wa* would suggest sarcasm quite unintended.

Yet a further word for "intelligent," though it is typically glossed as "intellectual, mental," is *chiteki*:

11. 頭がいいかどうかは別として、学生に知的好奇心さえあれば、授業はやはり楽しいですね。

Atama ga ii ka dō ka wa betsu toshite, gakusei ni chiteki–kōki-shin sae areba, jugyō wa yahari tanoshii desu ne.

Regardless of how "clever" they are, if students have intellectual curiosity, classes really are enjoyable, aren't they.

The last example suggests *Chiteki-nihongo-kaiwa* as my own preferred Japanese rendition of the title. With this preceding lexical analysis as an appetizer, we may now move on to the main course.

CHAPTER

I

Ideas and Theories

It is often suggested that the Japanese are a more practical than philosophical people, disinclined to both abstractness and contentiousness. Be that as it may, the language certainly abounds in Chinese borrowings for argument, reason, and theory. While one must avoid the appearance of being disputatious (理屈っぽい *rikutsuppoi*), developing the ability to "cross swords" in a discussion (議論で太刀打ちできる *giron de tachi-uchi dekiru*) is certainly one way to sound intelligent in Japanese.

This chapter focuses on just three short words that appear with particularly high frequency in discourse of a more abstract nature. These are: 論 *ron* "argument, theory, ism," 理 *ri* "reason, principle, truth," and 説 *setsu* "theory, view, statement," all of which are used in both isolated and compound form. As can be seen in the illustrative sentences, they can also be combined with each other. 論理説 *ronri-setsu*, for example, is "theory of logic," and, at least hypothetically, one can even speak of 理論説 *riron-setsu* "a theory about theories."

The key to understanding the meaning of the words is in their actual usage, not in the English glosses. While there is some degree of interchangeability, e.g., between *-ron* and *-setsu*, as seen below, the student must generally learn the various combinations as distinct, though not entirely idiosyncratic, lexical items.

Argument, Theory, Ism
論 RON

As a label for philosophies and ideologies, *-ron* corresponds to English "-ism," 論者 *-ronsha* to English "-ist":

有神論 (*yūshin-ron*) theism (exist-god-ism)

理神論 (*rishin-ron*) deism (reason-god-ism)

無神論 (*mushin-ron*) atheism (no-god-ism)

一神論 (*isshin-ron*) monotheism (one-god-ism)

多神論 (*tashin-ron*) polytheism (many-god-ism)

汎神論 (*hanshin-ron*) pantheism (everything-god-ism)

不可知論 (*fukachi-ron*) agnosticism (not-can-know-ism)

唯我論 (*yuiga-ron*) solipsism (only-self-ism)

唯物論 (*yuibutsu-ron*) materialism (only-thing-ism)

唯心論 (*yuishin-ron*) spiritualism (only-heart-ism)

相対論 (*sōtai-ron*) relativism (mutual-opposite-ism)

普遍論 (*fuhen-ron*) universalism (common-everywhere-ism)

絶対論 (*zettai-ron*) absolutism (sever-opposite-ism)

1. いくら貴方が道徳には普遍性があると主張しても、私は究極的*
   には相対論者です。

   *Ikura anata ga dōtoku ni wa fuhen-sei ga aru to shuchō shite mo, watashi wa kyūkyoku-teki ni wa **sōtai-ron**sha desu.*

   You can insist on the universality of morality as much as you want, but I am ultimately a relativist.

   * *kyūkyoku-teki*: in the end, ultimately

2. 多くの日本人は、無神論者というよりも、決まった宗教のない
   アニミストではないかと思います。

   *Ōku no nihon-jin wa, **mushin-ron**sha to iu yori mo, kimatta shūkyō no nai animisuto de wa nai ka to omoimasu.*

   Rather than call most Japanese atheists, I tend to regard them as animists, without a definite religion as such.

3. 進化論が確実な証拠に基づいているとは思いません。

   ***Shinka-ron** ga kakujitsu na shōko ni motozuite iru to wa omoimasen.*

   I don't think evolutionism (the theory of evolution) is based on any convincing evidence.

4. ジョージ・バークレーは物質の存在を否定したので、一種の唯
   心論者と言えるでしょう。

   *Jōji bākurē wa busshitsu no sonzai o hitei shita no de, isshu no **yuishin-ron**sha to ieru deshō.*

   As George Berkeley denied the existence of matter, one might say he was a kind of monistic spiritualist.

5. ヨーロッパの元共産国でも、マルクス・エンゲルスの弁証法的

唯物論を理解できる人は少なかったでしょう。

*Yōroppa no moto–kyōsan-koku de mo, marukusu-engerusu no benshō-hō–teki **yuibutsu-ron** o rikai dekiru hito wa sukunakatta deshō.*

Even in the former Communist countries of Europe, there must have been few people who could understand the dialectic materialism of Marx and Engels.

Ron can also refer to the discussion or study of something whose existence is not in question. 意味論 *imi-ron*, for example, means the "study of meaning," i.e., semantics, and 宇宙論 *uchū-ron* the "study of the universe," i.e., cosmology. Likewise, 日本人論 *nihon-jin–ron* is not a theory about whether the Japanese exist, such as would be the case with 宇宙人論 *uchū-jin–ron*, lit. "space-people-ism," but rather "study of / theorizing about the Japanese." Uneasiness about too much speculative 論 *ron* and not enough empirical 学 *gaku* may be reflected in the following proverb, in which the former appears by itself:

6. 論より証拠。
Ron yori shōko.
Instead of arguments, evidence.

In compounds, we find *ron* used initially as well as finally:

論法 (*ronpō*) line of argument (argument law)
三段論法 (*sandan-ronpō*) a syllogism (three-step argument law)
論理 (*ronri*) logic (discourse principle)
論争 (*ronsō*) controversy (discourse war) (+ *suru*)
論戦 (*ronsen*) verbal dispute (discourse fight)
論点 (*ronten*) the point at issue (arguing point)

7. 「全ての人間は死ぬべきものだ。ソクラテスは人間である。故に*彼は死ぬべきである」というのは、有名な三段論法です。
*"Subete no ningen wa shinu beki mono da. Sokuratesu wa ningen de aru. Yue ni kare wa shinu beki de aru" to iu no wa, yūmei na **sandan-ronpō** desu.*

"All men are mortal; Socrates is a man; therefore, Socrates is mortal" is a famous syllogism.

＊ *yue ni*: therefore, consequently (literary usage)

8. 山本先生は、新しい論理説を述べています。
*Yamamoto-sensei wa, atarashii **ronri-setsu** o nobete imasu.*

Professor Yamamoto is expounding a new theory of logic.

9. 自衛隊を湾岸戦争に派遣すべきだったかどうかという論争には巻き込まれたくない。

*Jiei-tai o wangan-sensō ni haken subeki datta ka dō ka to iu **ronsō** ni wa makikomaretaku nai.*

I don't want to get involved in the controversy of whether the Self-Defense Forces should have been sent to the Gulf War.

Ron is also combined with the bound form of the verb *suru* (*-jiru*) "do," meaning "to discuss":

10. 先生たちは日本の教育制度について論じています。

*Sensei-tachi wa nihon no kyōiku-seido ni tsuite **ronjite** imasu.*

The teachers are discussing the Japanese educational system.

As a final element, *ron* appears in such compounds as 議論 *giron* "argument, debate" [+ *suru*], 討論 *tōron* "debate" [+ *suru*], 反論 *hanron* "counterargument"[+ *suru*], 結論 *ketsuron* "conclusion"[+ *o dasu*], 空論 *kūron* "empty theory, speculation," 言論 *genron* "speech, discussion."

11. 恐竜の絶滅の原因については、議論が続いています。

*Kyōryū no zetsumetsu no gen'in ni tsuite wa, **giron** ga tsuzuite imasu.*

There is ongoing debate concerning the cause of the dinosaurs' extinction.

12. あんな確実な証拠には、反論は難しい。

*Anna kakujitsu na shōko ni wa, **hanron** wa muzukashii.*

Presenting counterarguments in the face of such convincing evidence is difficult.

13. アトランティス伝説についての新説が立てられたが、空論でしかない。

*Atorantisu-densetsu ni tsuite no shinsetsu ga taterareta ga, **kūron** de shika nai.*

A new theory has been proposed concerning the legend of Atlantis, but it's only empty speculation.

14. 言論の自由は、民主主義の基本的条件の一つです。

***Genron** no jiyū wa, minshu-shugi no kihon-teki–jōken no hitotsu desu.*

Freedom of speech is a basic condition for democracy.

Reason, Principle, Truth
理 RI

Ri, more generally known in the West by its original Chinese form (*li*), is sometimes called the East Asian equivalent of Greek *logos* "primeval principle" or, as in St. John's Gospel, "the Word." Unlike *logos* (or, for that matter, *setsu* and *ron*), *ri* is not derived from a metaphorical extension of a word for "speaking": in its original sense, it means "thread, texture." A similar image—physical and spatial as opposed to verbal—is seen in native Japanese 筋 *suji* "muscle, fiber, vein, texture, plot": *suji ga tōru* "logical," lit. "the fiber passes through."

15. 陰陽の理は、中国人の考え方に大きな影響を及ぼしました。

*In'yō no **ri** wa, chūgoku-jin no kangae-kata ni ōkina eikyō o oyoboshimashita.*

The Yin-Yang principle had an enormous influence on Chinese thinking.

16. 貴方の論点に道理が全くないわけではありませんが、私はどうしても納得できません。

*Anata no ronten ni **dōri** ga mattaku nai wake de wa arimasen ga, watashi wa dōshite mo nattoku dekimasen.*

Your argument is not without reason, but I remain unpersuaded.

論理 *ronri* "logic" literally means "discourse principle." If the elements are turned around 理論 *riron*, the meaning shifts to "theory, speculation." Thus, whereas 論理的 *ronri-teki* means "logical," 理論的 *riron-teki* merely means "theoretical."

17. 捕鯨問題を持ち出すとすぐ感情的になってしまいます。もっと論理的に考えなければなりません。

*Hogei-mondai o mochidasu to sugu kanjō-teki ni natte shimaimasu. Motto **ronri-teki** ni kangaenakereba narimasen.*

Whenever I bring up the whaling issue, you always become emotional. You must think more logically.

As if *ri* were not basic enough, 原理 *genri* literally means "fundamental/original principle." Other words in which *ri* is the noninitial element are 学理 *gakuri* "scholarly, scientific principle," 教理 *kyōri* "(religious) doctrine," 地理 *chiri* "geography," and 合理 *gōri* "rationality."

Adding adjectival formant 的 *teki* to 合理 *gōri* yields the word for "rational, reasonable, logical," though the word can also be used in the somewhat negative sense of "coldly, ruthlessly logical." 合理化 *gōri-ka* "rationalization" is typically used in the context of rationalizing or streamlining business enterprises. (The term for the common practice of inventing flimsy excuses or false justifications to hide a guilty conscience is 正当化する *seitō-ka suru*.)

18. 労働組合は、これ以上の合理化に大反対です。
*Rōdō-kumiai wa, kore ijō no **gōri-ka** ni dai-hantai desu.*
The union is strongly opposed to any further rationalization.

The negative nuances of *gōri-teki* might suggest that the Japanese prize irrationality, but the question boils down to one of usage. After all, in English as well, the colloquial meaning of "argument" is not "line of reasoning" but rather "dispute, quarrel." The same point can be made with regard to *rikutsuppoi* above.

Compounds with *ri* as the initial element include: 理由 *riyū* (*ri* + "cause") "reason, cause"; 理性 *risei* (*ri* + "nature, quality") "reason, reasoning power"; 理想 *risō* (*ri* + idea) "ideal"; 理解 *rikai* (*ri* + "analysis") "apprehend, comprehend." Note that whereas English "apprehend" and "comprehend" originally mean "catch" and "absorb" respectively, *rikai* suggests the opposite cognitive process, loosening, untying, or dissolving. One word for "intellect" is 理知 *richi*, suggesting reason combined with knowledge, cf. Introduction.

19. 佐々木先生の理論はどうしても理解できません。
*Sasaki-sensei no riron wa dōshite mo **rikai** dekimasen.*
I am completely unable to comprehend Professor Sasaki's theory.

20. 恵次郎さんは一流大学を卒業をしなかったし、有名な会社にも勤めていないけど、私にとってやはり理想的な主人です。
*Keijirō-san wa ichiryū-daigaku o sotsugyō shinakatta shi, yūmei na kaisha ni mo tsutomete inai kedo, watashi ni totte yahari **risō-teki** na shujin desu.*
Keijirō didn't graduate from a top-ranking university, and he doesn't work for a famous company either, but for me he is still the ideal husband.

Compounds with less transparent meanings are 理学 *rigaku*, which refers not to the "study of reason" but rather to the "physical sciences." 理髪 *rihatsu* does not mean "reasoning hair" but rather "barbering." 理事 *riji*, *ri* + "matter, affair," refers to a "director" or "trustee," especially of a company or university, cf. 理事

会 *riji-kai* "board of directors, trustees" and 国連安全保障理事国 *kokuren-anzen-hoshō-rijikoku* "member nation of the UN Security Council."

21. 佐藤さんはかなり有名な画家ですが、娘さんは、美術より化学に興味を持って、東京大学の理学部に入学しました。

*Satō-san wa kanari yūmei na gaka desu ga, musume-san wa, bijutsu yori kagaku ni kyōmi o motte, tōkyō-daigaku no **rigaku-bu** ni nyūgaku shimashita.*

Mr. Satō is a rather well-known painter, but his daughter took a greater interest in chemistry than art and entered the University of Tokyo's Faculty of Science.

22. 家内は団地の理事になった時以来、性格が変わったようです。

*Kanai wa danchi no **riji** ni natta toki irai, seikaku ga kawatta yō desu.*

Ever since she began serving on our condominium complex's board of directors, my wife seems to have undergone a change of personality.

Theory, View, Statement
説 SETSU

In Chinese, the meaning of 説 is "speak," and though the pronunciation of the word has changed from /siuet/ in the Tang Dynasty to /shuo/ in Modern Mandarin, that is still its primary sense. In Sino-Japanese, on the other hand, it usually has the more specific meaning of "explanation" or "theory," though a broader sense is suggested in 小説 *shōsetsu* "novel" (not "small theory"), cf. 短編小説 *tanpen-shōsetsu* "short story," and 伝説 *densetsu* "legend" (lit. passed-on tale).

23. 日本語の起源については、いろいろの説があります。

*Nihon-go no kigen ni tsuite wa, iroiro no **setsu** ga arimasu.*

Concerning the origins of Japanese, there are all sorts of theories.

24. 谷崎潤一郎の短編小説の中で、まだ英訳されていないものが多いようです。

*Tanizaki jun'ichirō no **tanpen-shōsetsu** no naka de, mada eiyaku sarete inai mono ga ōi yō desu.*

There seem to be many Jun'ichiro Tanizaki short stories that have yet to be translated into English.

It is in the sense of "expound" that we find *setsu* as an initial element in such Sino-Japanese words as 説明 *setsumei* "explanation" (lit. speak and clarify), 説教 *sekkyō* "sermon" (lit. clarify and teach), and 説得 *settoku* "persuasion" (lit. explain and gain). All of these can be verbalized with *suru*.

25. 担当医の説明によると、父の手術にはかなりの危険性が伴うということです。

*Tantō-i no **setsumei** ni yoru to, chichi no shujutsu ni wa kanari no kiken-sei ga tomonau to iu koto desu*

According to the attending physician, there is a high degree of risk in my father's operation.

26. かおりちゃんはお父さんを説得して、タバコをやめさせました。

*Kaori-chan wa otōsan o **settoku** shite, tabako o yamesasemashita.*

Kaori persuaded her father to give up smoking.

27. 貴方の論文には説得力がありません。もっと論理的にまとめてください。

*Anata no ronbun ni wa **settoku**-ryoku ga arimasen. Motto ronri-teki ni matomete kudasai.*

Your thesis isn't persuasive. Please organize it more logically.

28. 母からボーイフレンドのことでまたお説教を聞かされました。

*Haha kara bōifurendo no koto de mata **osekkyō** o kikasaremashita.*

I had to listen to another lecture from my mother today about my boyfriend.

Compounds in which *setsu* appears as a noninitial element include 仮説 *kasetsu* "hypothesis" (lit. temporary view), 学説 *gakusetsu* "(learned) theory," and 定説 *teisetsu* "(widely) accepted theory," illustrated above. *Setsu* overlaps somewhat with *ron* in meaning and usage. Instead of *teisetsu*, for example, one can say *teiron*, cf. *shinka-setsu* for *shinka-ron* "theory of evolution." The difference may roughly correspond to the contrast between theory and discussion/question in English.

29. 日本語の起源説はいろいろありますが、定説というものはないようです。

*Nihon-go no kigen-**setsu** wa iroiro arimasu ga, **teisetsu** to iu mono wa nai yō desu.*

There are all sorts of theories regarding the origin of the Japanese language, but there does not appear to be any generally accepted one.

In the sense of "speak" or "elucidate," *setsu* is found in 解説 *kaisetsu* "commentary," 論説 *ronsetsu* "discourse, leading article, editorial," and 社説 *shasetsu* "leading article, editorial."

30. ＮＨＫのニュース解説を見ているのは、大学生より社会人の方が多いに違いありません。

*NHK no nyūsu-**kaisetsu** o mite iru no wa, daigaku-sei yori shakai-jin no hō ga ōi ni chigai-arimasen.*

No doubt more adults watch NHK news analysis and commentary than do university students.

31. あの方は、20年間朝日新聞の論説委員でした。

*Ano kata wa, nijū-nenkan asahi shinbun no **ronsetsu**-i'in deshita.*

For twenty years he was an editorialist for the *Asahi Shimbun*.

32. 火曜日のニューヨーク・タイムズのチベットに関する社説には、中国大使館から強い反発がありました。

*Kayō-bi no nyūyōku-taimuzu no chibetto ni kansuru **shasetsu** ni wa, chūgoku-taishikan kara tsuyoi hanpatsu ga arimashita.*

There was a strong reaction from the Chinese Embassy to Tuesday's *New York Times* editorial regarding Tibet.

CHAPTER

II

Philosophy and Religion

The English proverb "One man's meat is another man's poison" is served up in Japanese as 甲の薬は乙の毒 *Kō no kusuri wa otsu no doku* "What is medicine to A may be poison for B." Such philosophical relativism seems to offer a certain universal appeal, to both pre-Socratic sophists (詭弁家 *kiben-ka*) and modern multiculturalists (多元文化論者 *tagen-bunka–ronsha*). Thus, whether you believe in the "marketplace of ideas" or the "battlefield of ideologies," it may be wise to walk armed with an adequate vocabulary.

We begin with three compound-formants: 主義 *shugi* "principle, -ism," 教 *kyō* "teaching," and 派 *ha* "faction, sect," with illustrations largely from the "international" world that Japan has known since the Meiji era. We then move on to more traditional, specifically "Japanese" terms.

Principle, Ism
主義 SHUGI

In the modern language, 主義 *shugi* "-ism" is indispensable, if not all-pervasive, ranging from 帝国主義 (*teikoku-shugi*) "imperialism" to マイホーム主義 (*maihōmu-shugi*) "family-first-ism." This quasi-suffix is relatively new, a coinage of the Meiji-era journalist Fukuchi Gen'ichirō as a translation for (Latinate) English "principle." The literal meaning of the compound might be explained as "guiding cause."

楽天主義 (*rakuten-shugi*) optimism (pleasant-heaven-ism)
悲観主義 (*hikan-shugi*) pessimism (sad-view-ism)
理想主義 (*risō-shugi*) idealism (principle-idea-ism)

浪漫主義 (*ro(o)man-shugi*) romanticism (wander-ramble-ism)

Despite the clever *jeu de mots* seen in the choice of characters here for "romanticism," the more common term today is ロマンチシズム *romanchishizumu*. Note that for the following three, 論 *ron* (see Chapter 1) may also be used:

観念主義 (*kannen-shugi*) idealism (viewing-thought-ism; as [German] school of philosophy)

経験主義 (*keiken-shugi*) empiricism (experience-ism)

実存主義 (*jitsuzon-shugi*) existentialism (actual-existence-ism)

Where theory shades into ideology or life style, 主義 *shugi* is more common than *ron*:

博愛主義 (*hakuai-shugi*) altruism (broad-love-ism)

菜食主義 (*saishoku-shugi*) vegetarianism (vegetable-eating-ism)

快楽主義 (*kairaku-shugi*) hedonism (delight-pleasure-ism)

個人主義 (*kojin-shugi*) individualism (single-person-ism)

利己主義 (*riko-shugi*) egoism (profit-self-ism)

Compounds of a more specifically political nature, e.g., 全体主義 *zentai-shugi* "totalitarianism," are treated in more detail in Chapter 3.

1. ベッカー先生は皮肉なことをよくおっしゃいますが、実際にはどこまでも理想主義者だと思います。

Bekkā-sensei wa hiniku na koto o yoku osshaimasu ga, jissai ni wa dokomade mo risō-shugisha da to omoimasu.

Professor Becker may make a lot of cynical remarks, but I think he is, in fact, a stubborn idealist.

2. レーニンによると、帝国主義は資本主義の最後の段階だそうです。

Rēnin ni yoru to, teikoku-shugi wa shihon-shugi no saigo no dankai da sō desu.

According to Lenin, imperialism is supposed to be the last stage of capitalism.

3. 渡辺先生はイギリスの経験主義者/論者の専門家ですが、最近ドイツの形而上学*についての本を編纂†しました。

Watanabe-sensei wa, igirisu no keiken-shugisha/-ronsha no senmon-ka desu ga, saikin doitsu no keiji-jō–gaku ni tsuite no hon o hensan shimashita.

Professor Watanabe is an authority on the English empiricists, but recently he edited a book about German metaphysics.

* *keiji-jō–gaku*: metaphysics (beyond-form-study). Note that whereas in English it is common to use "metaphysical" in the sense of "abstruse," the Japanese are more likely to say 抽象的 *chūshō-teki* "abstract."

† *hensan suru*: to edit in the sense of arrange and annotate an author's works (cf. 編集 *henshū*: "edit," to prepare a completed manuscript for publication)

4.「個人主義」と「利己主義」を区別することは、難しいですね。
"Kojin-shugi" to "riko-shugi" o kubetsu suru koto wa, muzukashii desu ne.

Distinguishing "individualism" and "egoism" is difficult, isn't it?

5. 近所の精肉店の由美子さんは、カリフォルニアに留学して、菜食主義者になってしまいました。
*Kinjo no seiniku-ten no yumiko-san wa, kariforunia ni ryūgaku shite, **saishoku–shugi**sha ni natte shimaimashita.*

Yumiko, the neighborhood butcher's daughter, went off to California to study and wound up a vegetarian.

主義 *shugi* is commonly used to derive new expressions, such as マイホーム主義 *maihōmu-shugi* above:

エリート主義 (*erīto-shugi*) elitism

管理主義 (*kanri-shugi*) managerialism

安全第一主義 (*anzen-dai'ichi-shugi*) safety-first-ism

厳罰主義 (*genbatsu-shugi*) martinetism (strict-punishment-ism)

Note that *shugi* is not used to describe physical or psychological ailments such as astigmatism (乱視 *ranshi*) or alcoholism アルコール依存症 (*arukōru–izon-shō*). Nor is it used in the sense of action or activity, e.g., baptism (洗礼 *senrei*), hypnotism (催眠術 *saimin-jutsu*), plagiarism (盗作 *tōsaku*, lit. stealing works). Used in a linguistic sense, -ism is translated as 語法 (*-gohō*), lit. "language law": ラテン語語法 *raten-go–gohō* "Latinism," 英語語法 *eigo-gohō* "Anglicism."

Worship and Teachings
教 KYŌ

Like *shugi*, Sino-Japanese 哲学 *tetsugaku* "philosophy" ("study of wisdom") is a Meiji-era loan translation, coined by 西周 Nishi Amane as an approximation of the Greek term. The word for "religion" (宗教 *shūkyō*), on the other hand, is an example of an old compound given a new meaning. Originally a Buddhist term, it first meant "worship and teachings" or "the teachings of worship"; later it was used as the equivalent of English "religion." 教 *kyō*, in turn, appears in the names of most religions, though the word for the native religion of Japan is an obvious exception: Shintō 神道 "the way of the gods."

ユダヤ教 (*yudaya-kyō*) Judaism
道教 (*dōkyō*) Taoism
儒教 (*jukyō*) Confucianism
ジャイナ教 (*jaina-kyō*) Jainism
仏教 (*bukkyō*) Buddhism
拝火教 (*haika-kyō*) Zoroastrianism
キリスト教 (*kirisuto-kyō*) Christianity
カトリック教 (*katorikku-kyō*) Catholicism
ギリシャ正教 (*girisha-seikyō*) Greek Orthodoxy
新教 (*shinkyō*) Protestantism
ヒンズー教 (*hinzū-kyō*) Hinduism
イスラム教 (*isuramu-kyō*) Islam or 回教 *kaikyō*
シーク教 (*shīku-kyō*) Sikhism
モルモン教 (*morumon-kyō*) Mormonism

To substitute -ist for -ism, one adds 徒 *-to* "follower, pupil":

キリスト教徒 (*kirisuto-kyōto*) Christian
ヒンズー教徒 (*hinzū-kyōto*) Hindu

In the Edo period, Christianity was described as 邪教 *jakyō* "evil (perverse) religion." 異教(徒) *ikyō(-to)*, lit. "alien religion (-ist)," on the other hand, generally suggests a Judeo-Christian or Islamic perspective, cf. English "pagan," "infidel." (Intra-religious dissenters are described as 異端者 *itan-sha* "heretics," though again typically in an Occidental context, so that for the Japanese, with their noted tendency toward philosophical and religious eclecticism [折衷主義 *setchū-shugi* "submit-to-the-middle-ism"], the fine distinction between pagans and heretics is easily lost.)

6. ミッションスクールを卒業した娘たちは洗礼を受けましたが、私自身はキリスト教徒ではありません。
*Misshon-sukūru o sotsugyō shita musume-tachi wa senrei o uke-mashita ga, watashi jishin wa **kirisuto-kyōto** de wa arimasen.*
My daughters were graduated from a mission school and were bap-

tized, but I myself am not a Christian.

7. 倫理や社会の問題を中心にする儒教を、キリスト教や仏教のように宗教と呼ぶべきかどうか分かりません。

*Rinri ya shakai no mondai o chūshin ni suru **jukyō** o, **kirisuto-kyō** ya **bukkyō** no yō ni **shūkyō** to yobu beki ka dō ka wakarimasen.*

I don't know whether one should consider Confucianism, which focuses on ethical and social questions, to be a religion in the same way that Christianity and Buddhism are.

8. 中国の道教と日本の禅宗はどういう関係があるのでしょうか。

*Chūgoku no **dōkyō** to nihon no zenshū wa dō iu kankei ga aru no deshō ka*

What is the relationship between Chinese Taoism and Japanese Zen?

9. キリスト教から分離した新宗教の多くは、やはりアメリカで誕生しました。

Kirisuto-kyō *kara bunri shita shin-**shūkyō** no ōku wa, yahari amerika de tanjō shimashita.*

Many of the new religions that are offshoots of Christianity originated, as one might expect, in America.

Note that such terms as nudism, sadism, and feminism tend to appear as loanwords: *nūdizumu* (*nūdisuto*), *sadizumu* (*sadisuto*), *feminizumu* (*feminisuto*). *Kanibarizumu* "cannibalism," on the other hand, may be more familiar in its Japanese form: 人食いの風習 *hitokui no fūshū* (lit. people-eating practice).

Factions and Sects
派 HA

Ha (派) is used to describe a variety of sects, factions, and schools.

古典派 (*koten-ha*) classicism
ロマン(浪漫)派(*roman-ha*) romanticism
印象派 (*inshō-ha*) impressionism
宗派 (*shūha*) (religious) sect, denomination
スンニ派 (*sunni-ha*) Sunnism (Sunnis)
シーア派 (*shīa-ha*) Shiism (Shiites)
右派 (*u-ha*) the Right, cf. 右翼 (*uyoku*) "right wing"
左派 (*sa-ha*) the Left, cf. 左翼 (*sayoku*) "left wing"
中道派 (*chūdō-ha*) moderate faction

保守派 (*hoshu-ha*) conservatives

改革派 (*kaikaku-ha*) reformists

急進派 (*kyūshin-ha*) radical reformists

過激派 (*kageki-ha*) extremists

トロツキー派 (*torotsukī-ha*) Trotskyists

10. 大学院に入る前は、印象派の画家にはあまり興味がありません
でした。

*Daigaku-in ni hairu mae wa, **inshō-ha** no gaka ni wa amari kyōmi
ga arimasen deshita.*

Before I entered graduate school, I wasn't particularly interested in
the impressionist painters.

11. イスラム教のシーア派は、イランでもイラクでも多数を占めて
いますが、イランと違って、イラクにはスンニ派の信者も多い
そうです。

*Isuramu-kyō no **shīa-ha** wa, iran de mo iraku de mo tasū o shimete
imasu ga, iran to chigatte, iraku ni wa **sunni-ha** no shinja mo
ōi sō desu.*

Shiites are the majority in both Iran and Iraq, but unlike Iran, Iraq
has many Sunnis as well.

12. 駅の前で老人を殴ったり蹴ったりした過激派の連中*は、警察
に逮捕されました。

*Eki no mae de rōjin o naguttari kettari shita **kageki-ha** no renchū
wa, keisatsu ni taiho saremashita.*

The (political) extremists who punched and kicked an old man in
front of the railway station have been arrested by the police.

* *renchū*: set, bunch (often derogatory)

派 (*ha*) is combined with 学 (*gaku*) "study, -logy" for the
names of schools or sects of philosophy:

プラトン学派 (*puraton-gakuha*) Platonists

デカルト学派 (*dekaruto-gakuha*) Cartesians

カント学派 (*kanto-gakuha*) Kantians

13. カント学派の観念論主義*をイギリスで広めたのは、スコット
ランド生まれのトーマス・カーライルです。

*Kanto-**gakuha** no kannen-ron–shugi o igirisu de hirometa no wa,
sukottorando-umare no tōmasu kārairu desu.*

It was the Scotsman Thomas Carlyle who disseminated Kantian
idealism in Britian.

The word "cynic," when used as an historical term referring
to the "dog-like" school of Greek philosophy, is 犬儒学派
kenju-gakuha "Cynics" (lit. dog Confucian school), but the

general term for a cynical person or one noticeably fond of irony is 皮肉屋 *hiniku-ya* "skin-flesh-person." *Hiniku* has come to be used in the general sense of "irony, sarcasm (from Greek, lit. flesh-tearing)." (On a cross-cultural note, it might be mentioned that the Japanese in general seem less inclined than Westerners to appreciate sarcasm, so that while you may think you are being wittily ironic, the Japanese may judge you as merely 意地悪 *ijiwaru* "mean and perverse.")

In referring to the Skeptics as a Greek school of philosophy, you should say 懐疑派 *kaigi-ha* "hold-in-doubt faction," but if you merely wish to say that you are "skeptical" about a particular idea or proposal, it is more common to say 疑問/疑いを持っています *gimon/utagai o motte imasu* "[I] have questions/doubts" than 懐疑的に見ている *kaigi-teki ni mite iru* "[I] take a skeptical view."

哲学 *tetsugaku* is not used in quite the same broad sense as English "philosophy," which, at least colloquially, can mean "(personal) policy, way of thinking." Whereas a Southern California fitness club proprietor may speak of his "body-building philosophy," one might refer to such in Japanese by the less lofty-sounding ボディービルの道 *bodībiru no michi* ("way …"). Recently, one hears personal views of life being referred to as (私の)哲学 *(watashi no) tetsugaku* "(my) philosophy," along with 人生観 *jinsei-kan* "life view," but if you want to say "My philosophy has always been to avoid between-meal snacks," it is better to say simply: 食間にものを食べないのが私の方針です *Shokkan ni mono o tabenai no ga watashi no hōshin* (= policy) *desu.*

14. 私の人生観を言いますと、結局「過ぎたるは猶及ばざるがごとし」ということになるでしょう。

*Watashi no **jinsei-kan** o iimasu to, kekkyoku "sugitaru wa nao oyobazaru ga gotoshi" to iu koto ni naru deshō.*

I suppose my philosophy of life comes down to "Going too far is the same as not going far enough." (from the *Analects of Confucius*; cf. Horace's *aurea mediocritas*, the golden mean)

Wordsworth may speak of "the years that bring the philosophic mind," but to speak of 哲学的な精神 *tetsugaku-teki na seishin* in Japanese smacks of translationese. More natural is 平静な心 *heisei na kokoro* "calm spirit."

15. 年をとり髪の毛が薄くなっても、平静な心を持ち続けられると

は限りません。

*Toshi o tori kami no ke ga usuku natte mo, **heisei na kokoro** o mochitsuzukerareru to wa kagirimasen.*

Advancing age and thinning hair will not necessarily give one enduring serenity.

Traditional Japanese Philosophical and Religious Terminology

日本の伝統的宗教・哲学用語　NIHON NO DENTŌ-TEKI SHŪKYŌ・TETSUGAKU YŌGO

Even more than the West, Japan may be a largely "secularized" (this-worldly) society. Everyday Japanese conversation is nonetheless replete with expressions reflecting Japan's religious and philosophical traditions, as illustrated in the following selection of words and idioms. We begin with 世俗 *sezoku* (lit. worldly ways), the mundane, secular world.

16. 野村さんはきわめて精神(主義)的なひとで、金もうけや出世といった世俗的なことに全く興味がありません。

*Nomura-san wa kiwamete seishin(-shugi)-teki na hito de, kanemōke ya shusse to itta **sezoku**-teki na koto ni mattaku kyōmi ga arimasen.*

Mr. Nomura is an extremely spiritually minded person who has no interest in mundane matters such as material wealth or social climbing.

Originally, 世俗 *sezoku* was a Buddhist term, referring to the division between the monastic and the mundane. In a broader modern sense, however, it refers to the general tendency in many societies today toward desacralization. Furthermore, just as with English "mundane" (lit. of this world), 世俗的 *sezoku-teki* is also used in a cultural sense, i.e., "unrefined, vulgar," though 通俗的 *tsūzoku-teki* (lit. passing through the ordinary) appears to be more common.

The dictionary will tell you that *sezoku-ka* means secularization, but more commonly the term refers to the popularization of an institution or custom once limited to aristocratic or other elite circles.

Other Buddhist expressions, many of them similarly "secularized," include: 他力本願 *tariki-hongan* "reliance on others for help." Literally "other-power-original vow," this refers originally to the concept of salvation by faith in the Amida Buddha, whose vow it is to save all sentient beings. In popular usage, the term tends to have a negative connotation.

17. 和子さんは困った時はいつも他力本願です。今度はいくら甘え
ようとしても助けないつもりです。

*Kazuko-san wa komatta toki wa itsumo **tariki-hongan** desu. Kondo wa ikura amaeyō to shite mo tasukenai tsumori desu.*

Whenever Kazuko gets into a jam, she always expects others to bail her out. This time no matter how much she babies up to me, I'm not going to help her.

自力 *jiriki* "self-power" is the logical opposite of the *tariki* concept. Note the *go* reading of 力 as *riki*, which is typical of such Buddhist terms, and the contrast with 独力 *dokuryoku*, lit. "lone power."

18. 妹は、親から一銭ももらわずに自力で（独力で）医者になりま
した。

*Imōto wa, oya kara issen mo morawazu ni **jiriki** de (dokuryoku de) isha ni narimashita.*

My younger sister became a doctor quite on her own, without taking a penny from our parents.

Other examples of words originating in Buddhism with full or partial *go* readings are:

地獄 (*jigoku*) hell
極楽 (*gokuraku*) Buddhist paradise
業 (*gō*) karma, deeds committed in a previous existence
建立 (*konryū*) founding, erection of a temple/shrine/tomb-stone
立往生 (*tachi-ōjō*) stalling, last stand (lit. to die standing; *ōjō* = to go to be reborn)
今生 (*konjō*) this (fleeting) world [ko⌐njō]
後生 (*goshō*) afterlife
根性 (*konjō*) disposition, nature, mentality, tenacity [ko⌐njō]
修行 (*shugyō*) training, novitiate, apprenticeship
苦界 (*kugai*) world of suffering, life of prostitution
畜生 (*chikushō*) bestial (form of) life, damn!
前世 (*zense*) previous existence

19. それは、運が悪いというよりやはり前世の業だろうと思います。
*Sore wa un ga warui to iu yori yahari **zense** no **gō** darō to omoimasu.*

I believe it's not so much a matter of bad luck as the result of mis-deeds from a previous existence.

You will hear older women say 後生だから *goshō da kara* as in the following:

20. 後生だから、お酒を飲みすぎないでください。
Goshō da kara, osake o nomisuginai de kudasai.
For the love of mercy, please don't drink too much.

21. 昨日の吹雪で、電車が立往生しています。
Kinō no fubuki de, densha ga tachi-ōjō shite imasu.
Because of yesterday's blizzard, trains are now snowbound.

22. 「島国根性」は、決して日本人に限られているとは言えない。
"Shimaguni-konjō" wa, kesshite nihon-jin ni kagirarete iru to wa ienai.
One can by no means say that "insularity" is limited to Japanese.

念仏(する) *nenbutsu (suru)* refers (literally) to prayer to the Buddha, while 念願(する) *nengan (suru)* has the vaguer meaning of "earnestly pray, wish, hope for."

23. 大学時代の初恋の人に再会することが宮本君の長年の念願です。
Daigaku-jidai no hatsukoi no hito ni saikai suru koto ga miyamoto-kun no naganen no nengan desu.
It has long been Miyamoto's fervent hope to be reunited with the girl he first fell in love with while a student at university.

If poor Miyamoto should break a leg on his way to their meeting, he may say 縁起が悪い *engi ga warui*, i.e., that he was unlucky or that the undertaking was ill-omened from the beginning. 縁 *en* is used by itself in the sense of "(karmic) relationship, fate," cf. 因縁 *innen*, lit. "cause and circumstance," in which, for phonological reasons, we find an "extra" *n* at the beginning of the second element.

24. 縁があって、同級生の妹と結婚しました。
En ga atte, dōkyū-sei no imōto to kekkon shimashita.
As fate would have it, I married the younger sister of a classmate of mine in school.

25. 彼と縁を切った理由は言いにくいが、女房を誘惑しようとしたことと関係ないわけではない。
Kare to en o kitta riyū wa iinikui ga, nyōbō o yūwaku* shiyō to shita koto to kankei nai wake de wa nai.

It's hard for me to say why I ended my friendship with him, but the fact that he tried to seduce my wife is not irrelevant.

　＊ *yūwaku*: to tempt, entice, allure, seduce

26. 宮本が初恋の友佳里ちゃんと去年の昆虫＊学会で再会したのは、
何かの因縁かも知れません。

*Miyamoto ga hatsukoi no yukari-chan to kyonen no konchū-gakkai de saikai shita no wa, nani ka no **innen** kamo shiremasen.*

I believe it was fate that Miyamoto met up again with Yukari, the first love of his life, at last year's entomology society meeting.

　＊ *konchū* (swarm + insect): an insect/insects; the more scientific equivalent of *mushi* (虫)

Not surprisingly, 縁 *en* is commonly used in association with marriage, as can be seen in such combinations as 縁談 *en-dan* "marriage proposal," 内縁 *naien* "common-law marriage," 離縁 *rien* "divorce," and 再縁 *saien* "remarriage." An unhappy relationship that somehow cannot be broken is vividly described as a 腐れ縁 *kusare-en* "rancid relationship."

The native Japanese reading of 縁 is *yukari*, as in 縁の者 *yukari no mono* "a relative, a person with whom one has some sort of ties." When such ties are cut, however, the Sino-Japanese reading is used: 縁切り *en-kiri*.

旦那 (or 檀那) *danna* "master," cf. *danna-san* "(your, her) husband," is originally from Sanskrit *danapati* "(rich) patron of religion." (Other Sanskrit elements which have entered Japanese via Chinese include 魔 *ma* "demon" [cf. 邪魔 *jama* "interference" and 魔法瓶 *mahō-bin* "large thermos bottle" lit. magic bottle], だるま [達磨] *daruma* "Bodhidharma, daruma [doll]," and 娑婆 *shaba* "this world, free society [e.g., as opposed to prison].")

27. 由美子さんの旦那さんは、中年になってからだるまのように太
ってしまった。

*Yumiko-san no **danna**-san wa, chūnen ni natte kara **daruma** no yō ni futotte shimatta.*

Yumiko's husband became fat as a daruma doll when he reached middle age.

28. 大変お邪魔いたしました。

*Taihen o**jama** itashimashita.*

Please excuse me for having disturbed you. (as either a polite way of saying good-bye or an apology for an interruption or disruption)

29. 娑婆はどうせ苦界です。
***Shaba** wa dōse **kugai** desu.*

When you come down to it, the world is nothing but a vale of tears.

30. 「娑婆の栄華は夢のゆめ。」（平家物語）
*"**Shaba** no eiga wa yume no yume."* (From *The Tale of the Heike*)

"The glory of this world is but a dream of a dream." (cf. the well-known Latin dictum *Sic transit gloria mundi!*)

31. 戦後の混乱の中で、まさにこの世は苦界と化した*。
*Sengo no konran no naka de, masa ni kono yo wa **kugai** to ka-shita.*

The chaotic aftermath of the war turned the normal misery of the world into genuine hell.

　　　* *ka-suru*: to be transformed into, turn into

The Sino-Japanese term for nirvana—the state of release not only from *kugai* but also from 輪廻 *rinne* (Sanskrit *samsara*), the endless cycle of birth, death, and rebirth—is 涅槃 *nehan*. A far more commonly understood Japanese word in this regard, as popularized in English through interest in Zen, is 悟り *satori*, derived from the verb 悟る (覚る) *satoru*, cf. adjective 聡い(敏い) *satoi* "clever, perceptive." Kenkyusha's *New Japanese-English Dictionary* offers the following example:

32. 仏陀はその菩提樹の下に座って悟りを開かれた。
*Butsuda wa bodai-ju no shita ni suwatte **satori** o hirakareta.*

Gautama sat under a banyan tree and experienced spiritual awakening.

Butsuda, another Indic word borrowed through Chinese, refers, of course, to Gautama, the historical Buddha.

33. 南無阿弥陀仏
Namu Amida Butsu
Hail Amida Buddha!

Combinations with *butsu* include the following:

仏像 (*butsuzō*) Buddhist statue
大仏 (*daibutsu*) great statue of the Buddha
石仏 (*sekibutsu*) stone Buddha
仏事 (*butsuji*) Buddhist memorial service
仏壇 (*butsudan*) Buddhist family altar
仏画 (*butsuga*) Buddhist painting
仏具 (*butsugu*) Buddhist (altar) articles
仏具屋 (*butsugu-ya*) Buddhist (altar) article shop
成仏 (*jōbutsu*) Nirvana, Buddhahood

念仏 (*nenbutsu*) prayer to the Buddha

34. おじいさんが亡くなるまで、家には仏壇がありませんでした。
*Ojiisan ga nakunaru made, uchi ni wa **butsudan** ga arimasen de-shita.*
Until my grandfather died, we didn't have a Buddhist altar in our house.

Another word for "Buddha," also written 仏, is *hotoke*, apparently an older borrowing via an Altaic language.

35. 知らぬが仏。(A Japanese proverb)
*Shiranu ga **hotoke**.*
Ignorance is bliss. (Lit. Not to know is to be a Buddha.)

In a profaner sense, *hotoke(-sama)* often refers to anyone who has recently died, specifically to the remains. A policeman, at least of the TV variety, may be heard to say:

36. これでとうとうあの男も仏になったというわけか。
*Kore de tōtō ano otoko mo **hotoke** ni natta to iu wake ka.*
So he's finally met his maker?

Note that *futsu*, the *kan* reading of 仏, refers now exclusively to France, e.g., 仏文学 *futsu-bungaku* "French literature."

The priest who will preside at the Buddhist funeral of the victim is, of course, a 坊主 *bōzu*, an older form of which is the source for English "bonze." Buddhist priests are usually referred to as お坊さん *obō-san*. Combinations with *bōzu* include: 坊主頭 *bōzu-atama*, lit. bonze head (i.e., hair cropped very short), and 三日坊主 *mikka-bōzu*, lit. three-day bonze, referring to the fickle and weak-willed, with their easily broken resolutions.

37. 主人はタバコをやめると何回も約束したことがあるけど、いつも三日坊主だわ。
*Shujin wa tabako o yameru to nankai mo yakusoku shita koto ga aru kedo, itsumo **mikka-bōzu** da wa.*
My husband has promised to quit smoking many times, but he never lasts long.

Words and expressions of Shintoist origin are far less pervasive or obvious than those deriving from Japan's Buddhist tradition. Here are provided a few examples.

The old word for "heaven" in Japanese is 天 *ame/ama-*, as in the name of 天照大神 Ama-terasu-ō-mikami "heaven-illuminating-great-revered-goddess," the sun deity whose grandson Ninigi no Mikoto descends to earth to found Japan. A humor- ously irreverent allusion to the myth is implied in the expres- sion 天下り *ama-kudari*, lit. coming down from heaven, refer- ring to high-level government bureaucrats retiring to assume high-paying positions in private industry.

Visitors to a Shinto shrine, e.g., the Grand Shrines of Ise (伊 勢大神宮 Ise Dai-Jingū), are called 参詣者 *sankei-sha* in Sino- Japanese. The native word for such pilgrimages is 詣 *mōde*, cf. 初詣 *hatsu-mōde* "first (New Year's) shrine visit." *Mōde* too has an extended, secularized use:

38. 様々な発展途上国が経済援助を求めて日本詣をする。
*Samazama na hatten-tojō-koku ga keizai-enjo o motomete nihon-**mōde** o suru.*
Various developing countries make their way to Japan in search of economic aid.

Those who find themselves making repeated appeals for such help may be described as doing お百度参り *ohyakudo-mairi* "going back and forth one hundred times to worship (and pray)." A similiar expression, also used in a secularized sense, is お百度を踏む *ohyakudo o fumu* "tread one hundred times," used metaphorically to describe repeated requests for favors.

Finally, nothing is more representative of at least one domi- nant theme in traditional Japanese religion and philosophy than 無常 *mujō*, lit. "no constancy," referring to the transitory nature of all things. The concept is suggested in some of the examples above, but the specific term is perhaps best known from the familiar words that begin 平家物語 *Heike monogatari* or *The Tale of the Heike*, the early thirteenth-century war romance, also cited in example 30:

39. 「祇園精舎の鐘の声、諸行無常の響あり。」
*"Gion-shōja no kane no koe, shogyō-**mujō** no hibiki ari."*
"The sound of the Gion temple bell echoes the impermanence of all things."

The idea itself has an echo in sayings in many cultures and languages, as in the pre-Socratic philosopher Heraclitus' famous dictum: *panta rhei*, widely known in Japanese by its more or less literal translation: 万物流転 *Banbutsu-ruten* "All things flow and turn."

Politics and Government

Anthropos physei politikon zoon. If Aristotle had been Japanese, he would have said: 人間は本来政治的動物である *Ningen wa honrai seiji-teki–dōbutsu de aru* "Human beings are by nature political creatures." Thus, while the sagacious foreigner should be prudent (用心深い *yōjin-bukai*) in expressing his or her personal political views (政見 *seiken*), a mark of an intelligent cosmopolite (世界人 *sekai-jin* or 国際人 *kokusai-jin*) is the ability to understand and discuss the workings of the body politic (国政 *kokusei*), both nationally and internationally. This chapter begins with basic political concepts, then moves on to vocabulary used more specifically to describe the Japanese system of government. We conclude with terms useful to readers wishing to know how to talk about the political system in their home countries.

Government
政　SEI

The old native Japanese term for "government" is *matsuri-goto* (政), which originally referred to the "worship of the gods." Sino-Japanese 政 *sei* comes from Ancient Chinese *chieng*, which first meant "make straight", a reminder of the spirit of Confucianism that entered Japan, along with the new language, some 1,500 years ago. In the following are illustrated some of the compounds using the word.

政治 (*seiji*) politics
政治家 (*seiji-ka*) politician
政権 (*seiken*) political power

政党 (*seitō*) political party

政策 (*seisaku*) policy

政府 (*seifu*) government

国政 (*kokusei*) government, statecraft

行政 (*gyōsei*) administration

内政 (*naisei*) domestic politics

外政 (*gaisei*) foreign (diplomatic) policy

為政者 (*isei-sha*) statesman (lit. doing-politics-person)

1. 一般的に政治家は、遠い未来ではなく次の選挙＊のことしか考えない。

Ippan-teki ni seiji-ka wa, tōi mirai de wa naku tsugi no senkyo no koto shika kangaenai.

Generally speaking, politicians think not of the distant future but rather of the next election.

＊ *senkyo* (choose + raise): election

2. 今回の選挙で、保守党＊が政権を失う可能性はほとんどないと思います。

Konkai no senkyo de, hoshu-tō ga seiken o ushinau kanō-sei wa hotondo nai to omoimasu.

In the upcoming election, I think there is very little chance that the Conservative Party will lose power.

＊ *hoshu-tō* (preserve-protect party): Conservative Party

3. サッチャー元首相は、1979年から1991年まで政権を握っていました。それは、近代イギリスで最も長く続いた政権です。

Satchā moto-shushō wa, sen-kyūhyaku-nanajūkyū-nen kara sen-kyūhyaku-kyūjūichi-nen made seiken o nigitte imashita. Sore wa kindai igirisu de mottomo nagaku tsuzuita seiken desu.

Former Prime Minister Thatcher was in power from 1979 to 1991. It was the longest government in modern British history.

Note that *seiken* can refer both to political power in general and to individual governments in particular.

政 *sei* is also used in the sense of "management":

家政 (*kasei*) housekeeping

家政婦(さん) (*kasei-fu[-san]*) housekeeper, cleaning lady

郵政 (*yūsei*) postal system

財政 (*zaisei*) (public) finance

4. 今の日本では、よい家政婦さんを見つけるのは大変です。

Ima no nihon de wa, yoi kasei-fu-san o mitsukeru no wa taihen desu.

In contemporary Japan, it is very hard to find good domestic help.

5. 父は郵政省に勤めていました。

*Chichi wa **yūsei**-shō ni tsutomete imashita.*

My father worked for the Ministry of Posts and Telecommunications.

6. 野党*がその財政法案†に反対するのは、当たり前でしょう。

*Yatō ga sono **zaisei**-hōan ni hantai suru no wa, atarimae deshō.*

It is only to be expected that the opposition parties will oppose the finance bill.

* *yatō*: opposition party/parties

† *hōan*: a bill (before the legislature)

An earlier pronunciation of 政 is *shō*, but it is now confined exclusively to 摂政 *sesshō* "regency," as in 摂政の宮 *sesshō no miya* "Prince Regent."

Forms of Government
政体 SEITAI

Both 政 *sei* and 政体 *seitai* function as suffixes for terms describing "forms of government":

民政 (*minsei*) civilian government
軍政 (*gunsei*) military government
共和政体 (*kyōwa-seitai*) republicanism
立憲政体 (*rikken-seitai*) constitutionalism
立憲君主政体 (*rikken-kunshu–seitai*) constitutional monarchy

More common, however, is 主義 *shugi* "-ism," whose use is also illustrated in the previous chapter.

民主主義 (*minshu-shugi*) democracy (people-master-ism)
独裁主義 (*dokusai-shugi*) despotism, dictatorship
全体主義 (*zentai-shugi*) totalitarianism
自由主義 (*jiyū-shugi*) (classical) liberalism
社会主義 (*shakai-shugi*) socialism
共産主義 (*kyōsan-shugi*) communism (common-property-ism)
軍国主義 (*gunkoku-shugi*) militarism

Still another word-cum-suffix is 制(度) *sei(do)* "system":

君主制 (*kunshu-sei*) monarchial system (prince-master system)

天皇制 *(tennō-sei)* (Japan's) Emperor system

封建制度 *(hōken-seido)* feudalism, feudal system (fief-building system)

憲法制度 *(kenpō-seido)* constitutionalism

共和制度 *(kyōwa-seido)* republicanism (common-harmony system)

議会制度 *(gikai-seido)* parliamentary system

連邦制度 *(renpō-seido)* federalism

7. 民主主義の発祥地*のギリシャは、1967年から1974年まで軍政下にありました。

Minshu-shugi no hasshō-chi no girisha wa, sen-kyūhyaku-roku-jūnana-nen kara sen-kyūhyaku-nanajūyo-nen made gunsei-ka ni arimashita.

Greece, the birthplace of democracy, lay under military rule from 1967 to 1974.

  * *hasshō-chi*: place where something first occurs; cradle, birthplace

8. 英国や日本は、立憲君主国です。

Eikoku ya nihon wa, rikken–kunshu-koku desu.

Britain and Japan are constitutional monarchies.

9. 民主政体は、共和政体と同じであるとは限りません。

Minshu-seitai wa, kyōwa-seitai to onaji de aru to wa kagirimasen.

The democratic form of government does not necessarily mean a republican form of government.

10. 戦争中の日本を、ナチス・ドイツやスターリンのソビエトのように「全体主義国」と呼ぶべきかどうかは、歴史家や政治学者がまだ論争している問題です。

Sensō-chū no nihon o, nachisu-doitsu ya sutārin no sobieto no yō ni "zentai-shugi–koku" to yobu beki ka dō ka wa, rekishi-ka ya seiji-gakusha ga mada ronsō shite iru mondai desu.

Whether wartime Japan should be characterized as "totalitarian" in the same sense as Nazi Germany or the Soviet Union under Stalin is an issue still being debated by historians and political scientists.

11. 永田先生は、先週日本の封建制度について大変勉強になる講義をなさいました。

Nagata-sensei wa, senshū nihon no hōken-seido ni tsuite taihen benkyō ni naru kōgi o nasaimashita.

Last week Professor Nagata gave a most informative lecture on Japan's feudal system.

12. 日本の議会制度は、明治時代に遡ります*。

Nihon no gikai-seido wa, Meiji-jidai ni sakanoborimasu.

Japan's parliamentary system goes back to the Meiji era.

   * *sakanoboru:* to go upstream; to go back in time; to trace to the past

13. 日本には、実際に一党独裁があると言われますが、そうした*
   見方は極端すぎると思いませんか。

*Nihon ni wa, jissai ni ittō-dokusai ga aru to iwaremasu ga, sōshita
mikata wa kyokutan-sugiru to omoimasen ka.*

They say that Japan has, in fact, a one-party dictatorship but don't
you find that view too extreme?

   * *sōshita:* that, that kind of, such a

The Major Organs of Japan's Governing Body
日本の政治形態　NIHON NO SEIJI-KEITAI

The following is a summary of the most important terms you
will need to know when discussing the workings of the three
major branches of Japan's governing body—executive, legislative, and judicial:

行政府 *(gyōsei-fu)* the Administration

   内閣 *(naikaku)* the Cabinet

   総理府 *(sōri-fu)* Prime Minister's Office

   法務省 *(hōmu-shō)* Ministry of Justice

   外務省 *(gaimu-shō)* Ministry of Foreign Affairs

   大蔵省 *(ōkura-shō)* Ministry of Finance

   文部省 *(monbu-shō)* Ministry of Education

   厚生省 *(kōsei-shō)* Ministry of Health and Welfare

   農林水産省 *(nōrin-suisan-shō)* Ministry of Agriculture, For-
      estry, and Fisheries

   運輸省 *(un'yu-shō)* Ministry of Transport

   郵政省 *(yūsei-shō)* Ministry of Posts and Telecommunica-
      tions

   労働省 *(rōdō-shō)* Ministry of Labor

   建設省 *(kensetsu-shō)* Ministry of Construction

   自治省 *(jichi-shō)* Ministry of Home Affairs

   内閣官房長官 *(naikaku–kanbō-chōkan)* Chief Cabinet Sec-
      retary

   総理府総務長官 *(sōri-fu–somu-chōkan)* Director General of
      the Prime Minister's Office

国会 *(kokkai)* the Diet

   参議院 *(sangi'in)* House of Councilors

参議院議長 (*sangi'in-gichō*) President of the House of Councilors

参議院議員 (*sangi'in-gi'in*) Member of the House of Councilors

衆議院 (*shūgi'in*) House of Representatives

衆議院議長 (*shūgi'in-gichō*) House Speaker

衆議院議員 (*shūgi'in-gi'in*) Representative

司法 (*shihō*) the Judiciary

最高裁判所 (*saikō–saiban-sho*) Supreme Court

最高裁(判所)長官 (*saikō-sai[ban-sho]–chōkan*) Chief Justice of the Supreme Court

最高裁判事 (*saikō-sai–hanji*) Supreme Court Justice

14. 日本の総理大臣は、アメリカの大統領*ほど権力†を持っていません。

*Nihon no **sōri-daijin** wa, amerika no daitōryō hodo kenryoku o motte imasen.*

Japan's prime minister does not wield power to the same extent as do US presidents.

* *daitōryō*: president (of a republic; formal head of a parliamentary government)
† *kenryoku*: power, authority, influence

15. 与党*である自民党の党大会で選ばれる総裁は、自動的に総理になります。

*Yotō de aru jimin-tō no tō-taikai de erabareru sōsai wa, jidō-teki ni **sōri** ni narimasu.*

The president of the ruling Liberal Democratic Party, chosen at the party convention, automatically becomes prime minister.

* *yotō*: ruling party

16. 官房長官が突然辞任した理由はまだ明らかになっていませんし、その内幕*を知っているのは、ほんのわずかな政治家に限られているでしょう。

***Kanbō-chōkan** ga totsuzen jinin shita riyū wa mada akiraka ni natte imasen shi, sono uchimaku o shitte iru no wa, honno wazuka na seiji-ka ni kagirarete iru deshō.*

The reason for the sudden resignation of the Chief Cabinet Secretary is still not clear, and those who do have the inside story are probably limited to a handful of politicians.

* *uchimaku*: "behind-the-scenes story"

17. 東大出身*の新任外務大臣は、外国語が話せません。

*Tōdai-shusshin no shinnin–**gaimu-daijin** wa, gaikoku-go ga hanasemasen.*

The newly appointed foreign minister, a University of Tokyo graduate, does not speak any foreign language.

＊ *shusshin*: provenance; i.e., place of birth, permanent residence, alma mater, former (principal) occupation, etc.

18. 群馬県の衆院議員だった従兄は、去年の選挙で落選＊してしまいました。

*Gunma-ken no **shūin-gi'in** datta itoko wa, kyonen no senkyo de rakusen shite shimaishita.*

My cousin, who was a member of the House of Representatives from Gunma Prefecture, was defeated in the last election.

＊ *rakusen*: electoral defeat

19. 参議院には、芸能界出身の議員が何人ぐらいいるでしょうか。

*Sangi'in ni wa, geinō-kai–shusshin no **gi'in** ga nannin gurai iru deshō ka.*

In the House of Councilors, how many members do you suppose originally were from the entertainment world?

20. 神奈川県の強盗殺人事件で死刑判決＊を受けた加藤正彦は、無実を主張して最高裁判所に上訴†しました。

*Kanagawa-ken no gōtō-satsujin-jiken de shikei-hanketsu o uketa katō masahiko wa, mujitsu o shuchō shite **saikō–saiban-sho** ni jōso shimashita.*

Masahiko Kato, sentenced to death in an armed robbery and homicide case in Kanagawa Prefecture, appealed to the Supreme Court, insisting on his innocence.

＊ *shikei-hanketsu*: death sentence
† *jōso*: appeal

21. 「最高裁判所は、一切の法律、命令、規則又は処分が憲法に適合する＊かしないかを決定する権限†を有する終審裁判所である。」(日本国憲法、第八十一条)

*"**Saikō–saiban-sho** wa, issai no hōritsu, meirei, kisoku mata wa shobun ga kenpō ni tekigō suru ka shinai ka o kettei suru kengen o yū-suru shūshin–saiban-sho de aru." (Nihonkoku-kenpō, dai-hachijūichi-jō)*

"The Supreme Court is the court of last resort with power to determine the constitutionality of any law, order, regulation or official act." (The Constitution of Japan, Article 81)

＊ *kenpō ni tekigō suru*: be in conformity with, agree with, the constitution; be constitutional
† *kengen*: (authorized limits of) power, authority

22. アメリカの最高裁判所は、憲法の解釈だけではなく、立法に関してもかなり積極的な役割＊を果たしています。日本の最高裁判所はそれほど権力を持っていません。

*Amerika no **saikō–saiban-sho** wa, kenpō no kaishaku dake de wa naku, rippō ni kanshite mo kanari sekkyoku-teki na yakuwari o hatashiteimasu. Nihon no **saikō–saiban-sho** wa, sore hodo* *kenryoku o motte imasen.*

The US Supreme Court plays a rather activist role, not only in the interpretation of the Constitution but also in the making of laws. Japan's Supreme Court does not wield such power.

❈ *sekkyoku-teki na yakuwari*: activist role

Under the authority of the 総理府 *sōri-fu* "Prime Minister's Office" are 庁 *chō* "agencies" and 委員会 *i'in-kai* "commissions," which include:

北海道・沖縄開発庁 (*hokkaidō-okinawa–kaihatsu-chō*) Hokkaido and Okinawa Development Agencies

経済企画庁 (*keizai-kikaku-chō*) Economic Planning Agency

防衛庁 (*bōei-chō*) Defense Agency

環境庁 (*kankyō-chō*) Environment Agency

The heads of these agencies (長官 *chōkan*) are cabinet ministers, but those of the following are not.

警察庁 (*keisatsu-chō*) National Police Agency

宮内庁 (*kunai-chō*) Imperial Household Agency (lit. palace-interior agency)

23. 国立水俣病研究センターは、環境庁に属しています。
*Kokuritsu–minamata-byō–kenkyū-sentā wa, **kankyō-chō** ni zoku-shite imasu.*

The National Institute for the Minamata Disease is part of the Environment Agency.

24. 宮内庁は、皇室に関する事務を担当しています。
Kunai-chō wa, kōshitsu ni kansuru jimu o tantō shite imasu.

The Imperial Household Agency is in charge of matters related to the Imperial Household.

公正取引委員会 (*kōsei-torihiki-i'inkai*) Fair Trade Commission

国家公安委員会 (*kokka-kōan-i'inkai*) National Public Safety Commission

Japanese Political Parties
日本の政党　NIHON NO SEITŌ

Political parties in Japan are more numerous—and less long-lived—than in many of the other advanced industrial democracies. The following is a list of those which are likely to be known to the great majority of Japanese—and to be still in existence when this book is published. (Note that the 日本社会党 *nihon–shakai-tō* has changed its English name from the "Japan Socialist Party" to the "Social Democratic Party of Japan.")

自由民主党 (*jiyū–minshu-tō*) Liberal Democratic Party

日本社会党 (*nihon–shakai-tō*) Social Democratic Party of Japan

公明党 (*kōmei-tō*) Clean Government Party

民主社会党 (*minshu–shakai-tō*) Democratic Socialist Party (often abbreviated as 民社党 *minsha-tō*)

日本共産党 (*nihon–kyōsan-tō*) Japan Communist Party

与党 (*yotō*) party in power

野党 (*yatō*) opposition party

25. 自由民主党は、1955年に自由党と日本民主党が合わさって＊結成†された保守党で、それ以来日本の与党です。

Jiyū–minshu-tō wa, sen-kyūhyaku-gojūgo-nen ni jiyū-tō to minshu-tō ga awasatte kessei sareta hoshu-tō de, sore irai nihon no yotō desu.

The Liberal Democratic Party is a conservative party, born of the amalgamation of the Liberal Party and the Democratic Party in 1955 and, since then, Japan's ruling party.

＊ *awasaru*: to come together, combine
† *kessei*: form

26. 日本社会党は、たびたび「万年野党」と呼ばれます。

Nihon–shakai-tō wa, tabitabi "mannen-yatō" to yobaremasu.

The Social Democratic Party of Japan is often called the "permanent opposition party."

27. 公明党と創価学会との関係を説明してください。

Kōmei-tō to sōka-gakkai to no kankei o setsumei shite kudasai.

Please explain the relationship between the Clean Government Party (Kōmei-tō) and Sōka-gakkai.

28. 民社党は、1959年に日本社会党を脱党した穏健派＊です。

Minsha-tō wa, sen-kyūhyaku-gojūkyū-nen ni nihon–shakai-tō o dattō shita onken-ha desu.

The Democratic Socialist Party originated in a moderate faction that split off from the Japan Socialist Party in 1959.

＊ *onken-ha*: moderate faction

29. 日本共産党がどの程度マルクス・レーニン主義を否定しているかは、だれも分かりません。

Nihon–kyōsan-tō ga dono teido marukusu-rēnin–shugi o hitei shite iru ka wa dare mo wakarimasen.

No one knows to what extent the Japan Communist Party has dis-
avowed Marxism-Leninism.

Local Japanese Administrative Bodies
日本の自治体　NIHON NO JICHI-TAI

Jichi-tai literally means "self-governing body," a somewhat
misleading term in Japan's highly centralized system, referring
to local government. At the highest level, there are forty-seven
administrative units, consisting of forty-three 県 *ken* "prefectures," one 道 *dō* "province" (i.e., Hokkaidō), one 都 *to* "metropolis" (i.e., Tokyo), and two 府 *fu* "municipal prefectures"
(i.e., Kyoto and Osaka). Below these are 市 *shi* "cities," 町
machi/-chō "towns," and 村 *mura/-son* "villages." (Municipalities are also grouped into 郡 *gun* "districts" or "sub-pre-
fectures," but these have no local government functions.) The
large cities are divided into 区 *ku* "wards," within which there
are 町 *chō* "municipal districts," an administrative unit also
used in the smaller cities.

県知事 (*ken-chiji*) governor (of any of the forty-three prefec-
　　tures called *ken*)

道知事 (*dō-chiji*) governor (of Hokkaido)

都知事 (*to-chiji*) governor (of Tokyo)

府知事 (*fu-chiji*) governor (of either Kyoto or Osaka)

武蔵野市市長 (*musashino-shi–shichō*) Mayor of Musashino

港区区長 (*minato-ku–kuchō*) Minato Ward Chief

南町町長 (*minami-machi–chōchō*) Head of Minami Munici-
　　pal District

山崎村村長 (*yamazaki-mura-sonchō*) Yamazaki Village
　　Chief

Cities, towns, wards, and villages all have their 議会 *gikai*
"assemblies" and 議員 *gi'in* "assembly representatives."

市議会(議員) (*shi-gikai[–gi'in]*) city assembly (representative)

町議会(議員) (*chō-gikai[–gi'in]*) town assembly (representa-
　　tive)

区議会(議員) (*ku-gikai[–gi'in]*) ward assembly (represen-
　　tative)

村議会(議員) (*son-gikai[–gi'in]*) village assembly (representative)

Administrative offices for such purposes as the notification of deaths, marriages, and divorces are either 役所 (*yakusho*) or 役場 (*yakuba*), the one being used for municipalities and wards, the other for towns and villages.

市役所 (*shi-yakusho*) municipal office
区役所 (*ku-yakusho*) ward office
町役場 (*machi-yakuba*) town office
村役場 (*mura-yakuba*) village office

30. 私が初めて日本に来た時、東京都知事は美濃部さんでした。その後は、鈴木さんになりました。

*Watashi ga hajimete nihon ni kita toki, tōkyō-**to-chiji** wa minobe-san deshita. Sono ato wa, suzuki-san ni narimashita.*

When I first came to Japan, Mr. Minobe was the governor of Tokyo. Later came Mr. Suzuki.

31. 先月の市議会の選挙で当選した村上さんは、うちの子供たちが通っていた小学校の校長先生でした。

*Sengetsu no **shi-gikai** no senkyo de tōsen shita murakami-san wa, uchi no kodomo-tachi ga kayotte ita shōgakkō no kōchō-sensei deshita.*

Mr. Murakami, who was elected in last month's municipal assembly election, was the principal of the primary school our children attended.

32. 外国人登録証明書を紛失して*しまったので、これから市役所に行きます。

*Gaikoku-jin-tōroku-shōmeisho o funshitsu shite shimatta no de, kore kara **shi-yakusho** ni ikimasu.*

I've lost my alien registration certificate, so I'm now going to the municipal office.

* *funshitsu suru*: mislay, misplace, lose

International Politics
国際政治　KOKUSAI-SEIJI

As non-Japanese are often called upon to describe the political system of their native countries, we conclude with a selected list of those political institutions and offices. Some terms, e.g., 議会 *gikai* have general applicability, so that the アメリカ議会 *amerika-gikai* refers to the US Congress, 英国議会 *eikoku-gikai* to the British Parliament, ドイツ議会 *doitsu-gikai* to the German Bundestag, and イスラエル議会 *isuraeru-gikai* to the Israeli Knesset.

連合王国 *rengō-ōkoku* the United Kingdom
　下院 (*ka'in*) House of Commons
　上院 (*jōin*) House of Lords
　首相 (*shushō*) Prime Minister
　保守党 (*hoshu-tō*) Conservative Party
　労働党 (*rōdō-tō*) Labour Party
　社会民主党 (*shakai–minshu-tō*) Social-Democratic Party

　州 (*shū*) county, e.g., ケント州 (*kento-shū*) Kent
　島 (*tō*) isle (of), e.g., マン島 (*man-tō*) Isle of Man

カナダ連邦 *kanada-renpō* the Dominion of Canada
　上院 (*jōin*) Senate
　下院 (*ka'in*) House of Commons
　総督 (*sōtoku*) Governor General
　首相 (*shushō*) Prime Minister
　進歩保守党 (*shinpo–hoshu-tō*) Progressive Conservative
　　Party
　自由党 (*jiyū-tō*) Liberal Party

　州 (*shū*) province, e.g., オンタリオ州 (*ontario-shū*) Ontario
　準州 (*junshū*) territory, e.g,. ユーコン準州 (*yūkon-junshū*)
　　Yukon Territory

オーストラリア連邦 *ōsutoraria-renpō* the Commonwealth
　of Australia
　上院 (*jōin*) Senate
　下院 (*ka'in*) House of Representatives
　総督 (*sōtoku*) Governor General
　首相 (*shushō*) Prime Minister
　自由党 (*jiyū-tō*) Liberal Party
　国民党 (*kokumin-tō*) National Party
　労働党 (*rōdō-tō*) Labour Party
　民主労働党 (*minshu–rōdō-tō*) Democratic Labour Party
　州 (*shū*) province (state), e.g., タスマニア州 (*tasumania-
　　shū*) Tasmania
　準州 (*junshū*) territory, e.g., 北部の準州 (*hokubu no
　　junshū*) Northern Territory

アメリカ合衆国 *amerika-gasshūkoku* the United States of
　America

行政長官 (gyōsei-chōkan) chief executive = 大統領 (dai-tōryō) president

下院 (ka'in) House of Representatives

上院 (jōin) Senate

共和党 (kyōwa-tō) Republican Party

民主党 (minshu-tō) Democratic Party

州 (shū) state, e.g., ニューヨーク州 (nyūyōku-shū) New York State

郡 (gun) county, e.g., セント・ローレンス郡 (sento-rōrensu-gun) St. Lawrence County

33. ミス・ホワイトヘッドが保守党の代表として議会選挙に出馬する*という噂を聞いていますが、ほんとうでしょうか。

*Misu-howaitoheddo ga **hoshu-tō** no daihyō to shite gikai-senkyo ni shutsuba suru to iu uwasa o kiite imasu ga, hontō deshō ka.*

I've been hearing a rumor that Miss Whitehead is going to stand as a Conservative candidate in the parliamentary elections. Is it true?

* shutsuba suru: stand for election

34. 労働党による*左翼的影響は、近年弱まったそうです。

***Rōdō-tō** ni yoru sayoku-teki-eikyō wa, kinnen yowatta sō desu.*

Left-wing influence emanating from the Labour Party is said to have weakened in recent years.

* ni yoru: by (through the agency or action of)

35. カナダのケベック州の面積は、日本の2倍か3倍と言いますが、人口は700万人にもなりません。

*Kanada no kebekku-**shū** no menseki wa, nihon no nibai ka sanbai to iimasu ga, jinkō wa nanahyaku-man–nin ni mo narimasen.*

Canada's Quebec Province is two or three times larger than Japan in area, but its population does not reach seven million.

36. オーストラリアのホーク元首相は、労働党ですか。

*Ōsutoraria no hōku–moto-shushō wa **rōdō-tō** desu ka.*

Is Australia's former Prime Minister Hawke a member of the Labour Party?

37. オーストラリアの首都は、東南部にあるキャンベラ市です。

Ōsutoraria no shuto wa, tōnan-bu ni aru kyanbera-shi desu.

Australia's capital is Canberra, located in the Southeast.

38. アメリカには政党がたくさんありますが、実際には共和党と民主党が政権を交替するという二大政党制*になっています。

*Amerika ni wa seitō ga takusan arimasu ga, jissai ni wa **kyōwa-tō** to **minshu-tō** ga seiken o kōtai suru to iu ni–dai-seitō-sei ni natte imasu.*

There are many political parties in the United States, but the practical reality is that there is a two-party system, in which the Republicans and Democrats alternately hold power.

＊ *ni–dai-seitō-sei*: two-party system

39. スミス上院議員は、内政＊より外交†に興味を持っているようです。

Sumisu–jōin-gi'in wa, naisei yori gaisei ni kyōmi o motte iru yō desu.

Senator Smith seems to be more interested in foreign policy than in domestic policy.

＊ *naisei*: domestic politics
† *gaikō*: foreign policy

CHAPTER

IV

The Fine Arts, Humanities, and Social Sciences

It is often said that for the Greeks, arts, sciences, crafts, and trades were one, all contained in the single concept of *techne*. Not coincidentally, again thanks in part to Meiji-era word-smiths, Sino-Japanese 術 *jutsu* has a similarly broad meaning, appearing in compounds ranging from 美術 *bijutsu* "(fine) art" and 技術 *gijutsu* "technology" (lit. skill-art) to 催眠術 *saimin-jutsu* "hypnotism," 魔術 *majutsu* "witchcraft," and 造園術 *zōen-jutsu* "landscape gardening."

Jutsu, like *techne*, refers more to practice than to theory, in contrast to 学 *gaku* "study, knowledge, (branch of) learning." 美術 *bijutsu*, for example, refers to the beaux-arts, 美学 *bigaku* to aesthetics, i.e., "the study of the beautiful." *Gaku* is in this respect like Greek *mathema*, so that the Sino-Japanese equivalent of a "polymath"—from Greek *polymatheus* "knowing much"—is, in its original meaning, a 大学者 *dai-gakusha* (now replaced by 博学な人 *hakugaku na hito* "person of broad knowledge").

In this and the following chapter, we shall look at words from the world of learning, divided between the fine arts, the humanities, and the social sciences (文系 *bunkei*) on the one hand, the natural sciences (理系 *rikei*) on the other. We begin with more examples of *jutsu* and *gaku*, adding to them a third Sino-Japanese word, 芸 *gei*, which refers somewhat more specifically to "craft" in the sense of "trade." We then turn to selected examples of terms from six representative fields within the liberal arts: the beaux-arts, music, literature, linguistics, history, and sociology. Though some of these, particularly in linguistics, may be of greater interest to specialists, the great majority are likely to turn up in "intelligent" conversation as well.

Art, Knowledge, and Crafts
術・学・芸 JUTSU, GAKU, GEI

学術 (*gakujutsu*) learning, arts and sciences

芸術 (*geijutsu*) the arts

美術 (*bijutsu*) fine arts

戦術 (*senjutsu*) (military) tactics

話術 (*wajutsu*) (art of) storytelling/conversation

武術 (*bujutsu*) martial arts

医術 (*ijutsu*) the practice of medicine (but see below)

手術 (*shujutsu*) (surgical) operation

柔術 (*jūjutsu*) jujitsu (lit. the soft art; but see below)

呪術 (*jujutsu*) incantation, sorcery

鍼術 (*shinjutsu*) acupuncture

美容術 (*biyō-jutsu*) cosmetology

腹話術 (*fukuwa-jutsu*) ventriloquism

When English-speakers use "technique" as a synonym for "trick," they come close to expressing the ambivalence that Japanese-speakers have toward *jutsu*. Modern doctors wince when they hear their profession referred to as 医術 *ijutsu*, and adepts of the "soft art" prefer 柔道 *jūdō* "judo," the name by which it was first called by 嘉納治五郎 Kanō Jigorō (1860–1938).

1. 江戸時代にも、蘭学*を通して西洋の医術について知識を得ていた日本人がいました。

*Edo-jidai ni mo, rangaku o tōshite seiyō no **ijutsu** ni tsuite chishiki o ete ita nihon-jin ga imashita.*

Even in the Edo period, there were Japanese, who, via "Dutch studies," had knowledge of Western medicine.

* *rangaku*: Dutch studies

2. 「医術の修得には人生が短すぎる。」

*"**Ijutsu** no shūtoku ni wa jinsei ga mijika-sugiru."*

Life is too short for the task of mastering the art of medicine.

This is the original meaning of a comment by Hippocrates, whose Latin form is Seneca's well-known *ars [techne] longa, vita brevis* "Art is long, life is short."

3. 父は3年前に癌だと診断されて手術を受けた時、手遅れだと医者
に言われましたが、奇跡的に回復してきたようです。

*Chichi wa sannen mae ni gan da to shindan sarete **shujutsu** o
uketa toki, te-okure da to isha ni iwaremashita ga, kiseki-teki ni
kaifuku shite kita yō desu.*

When my father was diagnosed three years ago with cancer and
operated on, we were told by the doctor that it was too late to
save him, but miraculously he seems to have recovered.

4. 1831年に死去したプロイセンのクラウゼウィッツ将軍は、西洋
の最も有名な軍事理論家あるいは戦術家です。

*Sen-happyaku-sanjūichi-nen ni shikyo shita puroisen no kurauze-
wittsu-shōgun wa, seiyō no mottomo yūmei na gunji-rinronka
aruiwa **senjutsu**-ka desu.*

General (Karl von) Clausewitz of Prussia, who died in 1831, is the
West's best known military theoretician or strategist.

5. 和幸さんは、会社をやめて鍼術を習い、スペイン人の奥さんと
一緒にバルセロナに住んで、鍼医者として大成功しました。

*Kazuyuki-san wa, kaisha o yamete **shinjutsu** o narai, supein-jin no
okusan to issho ni baruserona ni sunde, hari-isha to shite dai-
seikō shimashita.*

Quitting his company, Kazuyuki studied acupuncture, settled in
Barcelona with his Spanish wife, and became quite successful as
an acupuncturist.

   Jutsu appears as the initial element in a limited number of
compounds and may also be used by itself.

6. 奥さんが亡くなった後、金田さんは女性詐欺師の術策*に陥って
2億円を取られました。

*Okusan ga nakunatta ato, kaneda-san wa josei–sagi-shi no **jussaku** ni ochiitte nioku-en o toraremashita.*

After his wife died, Mr. Kaneda fell for the scheme of a female con
artist, who took him for ¥200 million.

   * *jussaku*: artifice, ruse (lit. craft-sheme)

7. あなたのように処世*(の)術を知っている人は、今の問題をどう
にかして解決できるはずです。

*Anata no yō ni shosei (no) **jutsu** o shitte iru hito wa, ima no mondai o dō ni ka shite kaiketsu dekiru hazu desu.*

Someone as wise as you are to the ways of the world ought to be
able to come up with some way of solving the current problem.

   * *shosei*: to make one's way in society

   Gaku may likewise appear by itself and, more often than
jutsu, turns up in initial position as well.

8. 渡辺先生は幼少*のころより学を志して[†]大仏文学者になりました。

*Watanabe-sensei wa yōshō no koro yori **gaku** o kokorozashite dai-futsu-bungaku-sha ni narimashita.*

Professor Watanabe had his mind set on learning from the time he was small and became a renowned French literature scholar.

 * *yōshō*: childhood, early years
 † *kokorozasu*: aspire to

   学問 (*gakumon*) learning, scholarship
   学園 (*gakuen*) educational institution, academy
   学院 (*gakuin*) academy
   学校 (*gakkō*) school
      小学校 (*shōgakkō*) primary school
      中学校 (*chūgakkō*) middle school
      高(等学)校 (*kō[tō-gak]kō*) (senior) high school
      大学 (*daigaku*) university
      大学院 (*daigaku-in*) graduate school
   学部 (*gakubu*) (university) college, faculty
   学士号 (*gakushi-gō*) bachelor's degree
   学位 (*gakui*) (higher) academic degree
      修士 (*shūshi*) MA
      博士 (*hakushi*) PhD (cf. 博士号 *hakase-gō*)
   学費 (*gakuhi*) school expenses
   学歴 (*gakureki*) school career
   学名 (*gakumei*) scientific name
   学芸 (*gakugei*) arts and sciences

9. 谷口先生は学問的には優秀な人物かもしれませんが、どう見ても人間味が足りないような気がします。

*Taniguchi-sensei wa **gakumon**-teki ni wa yūshū na jinbutsu kamo shiremasen ga, dō mite mo ningen-mi ga tarinai yō na ki ga shimasu.*

Professor Taniguchi may be an outstanding person as a scholar, but he seems somehow lacking in a sense of humanity.

10. プラトンの設立した*紀元[†]前4世紀のアカデミー（学園）は、アテネに近い小さな森にあったそうです。

*Puraton no setsuritsu shita kigen-zen yon-seiki no akademī (**gakuen**) wa, atene ni chikai chiisana mori ni atta sō desu.*

Plato's Academy of the fourth century B.C. is said to have been located in a grove not far from Athens.

 * *setsuritsu suru*: to found, establish
 † *kigen*: an epoch or the first year in any epoch; here refering to the Western calendar

11. 日本は未だに高級官吏への道は有名大学を出ることから始まる
　　という学歴社会です。

*Nihon wa imada ni kōkyū-kanri e no michi wa yūmei-daigaku o
deru koto kara hajimaru to iu **gakureki**-shakai desu.*

Japan even today is a "name-school"-conscious society, in which
the way to a career as a high-level bureaucrat passes through
the gates of a famous university.

12. 家の長女は東京学芸大学で国文学を、次女は東京芸術大学で音
　　楽を専攻しています。

*Uchi no chōjo wa tōkyō-**gakugei**-daigaku de kokubun-gaku o, jijo
wa tōkyō-**geijutsu**-daigaku de ongaku o senkō shite imasu.*

Our eldest daughter is specializing in Japanese literature at Tokyo
Gakugei [Arts and Sciences] University; our second daughter
is specializing in music at Tokyo University of Fine Arts.

13. 原則として、アメリカの大学で教授になるには博士号を取得し
　　て＊いなければなりません。

*Gensoku to shite, amerika no daigaku de kyōju ni naru ni wa
hakase-gō o shutoku shite inakereba narimasen.*

As a rule, one must hold a doctoral degree in order to become a
professor at an American university.

＊ *shutoku*: acquire, gain

14. 日本の大学の人文学部では、教員が博士課程を終えないまま採
　　用されるのが普通です。

*Nihon no daigaku no jinbun-**gakubu** de wa, kyōin ga **hakushi**-
katei o oenai mama saiyō-sareru no ga futsū desu.*

In the college of humanities at Japanese universities, it is normal
for teaching personnel to be hired without completion of the
doctoral course.

15. 鰹（かつお）の学名は katsuwonus pelamis です。

*Katsuo no **gakumei** wa katsuwonus pelamis desu.*

The scientific name for the [oceanic] bonito is *katsuwonus pelamis*.

Gaku commonly appears as a suffix for names of academic
disciplines:

哲学 (*tetsugaku*) philosophy
文学 (*bungaku*) literature
言語学 (*gengo-gaku*) linguistics
論理学 (*ronri-gaku*) logic
心理学 (*shinri-gaku*) psychology
人類学 (*jinrui-gaku*) anthropology
歴史学 (*rekishi-gaku*) history

歴史学 (*rekishi-gaku*) history

法学 (*hōgaku*) law

経済学 (*keizai-gaku*) economics

社会科学 (*shakai-kagaku*) social sciences

政治学 (*seiji-gaku*) political science

工学 (*kōgaku*) engineering

生物学 (*seibutsu-gaku*) biology

植物学 (*shokubutsu-gaku*) botany

動物学 (*dōbutsu-gaku*) zoology

天文学 (*tenmon-gaku*) astronomy

地質学 (*chishitsu-gaku*) geology

地理学 (*chiri-gaku*) geography

医学 (*igaku*) medicine

To all of these words, a further suffix, 者 *-sha*, is applicable, yielding the equivalents of English philosopher, literary scholar (or writer), linguist, logician, psychologist, anthropologist, historian, economist, etc.

16. 古代ギリシャの"logistike"は、論理学ではなく算数の意味を持っていました。"Mathetes"は、数学者ではなく生徒でした。

*Kodai-girisha no "logistike" wa, **ronri-gaku** de wa naku sansū no imi o motte imashita. "Mathetes" wa, **sūgaku-sha** de wa naku seito deshita.*

Logistike in Ancient Greece did not signify the art of logic but rather arithmetic; a *mathetes* was not a mathematician but rather a pupil.

17. 須美子さんの婚約者が東大法学部を出たって、ほんとうなんですか。

*Sumiko-san no kon'yaku-sha ga tōdai–**hōgaku-bu** o deta tte, hontō nan desu ka.*

Is it true what I hear, that Sumiko's fiance is a graduate of the Law Faculty of Tokyo University?

18. 弟は慶応大学の工学部大学院を卒業して、コンピュータ会社に入りました。

*Otōto wa keiō-daigaku no **kōgaku-bu**–daigaku-in o sotsugyō shite, konpyūta-gaisha ni hairimashita.*

My younger brother graduated from Keio University's Graduate School of Engineering and entered a computer company.

If *gaku* suggests theoretical knowledge—staid, dignified, and somewhat remote—*gei*, even more than *jutsu*, suggests

文芸 (*bungei*) literary arts

工芸 (*kōgei*) industrial arts

陶芸 (*tōgei*) ceramic arts

民芸 (*mingei*) folk art

手芸 (*shugei*) handicrafts

演芸 (*engei*) performing arts

曲芸 (*kyokugei*) acrobatics

芸人 (*geinin*) artist, performer

芸者 (*geisha*) geisha

芸能界 (*geinō-kai*) entertainment world, show business

19. 「文藝春秋」は広い読者層をもってきました。

*"**Bungei**-shunjū" wa hiroi dokusha-sō o motte kimashita.*

Bungei-Shunjū [lit. Literary Spring and Autumn] has acquired a broad readership.

20. 主人は工芸研究所に勤めております。

*Shujin wa **kōgei**–kenkyū-jo ni tsutomete orimasu.*

My husband works for a polytechnic institute.

21. 大野監督の映画が前衛*芸術か、ただのポルノかという問題を、映画評論家だけに任せようという意見には反対です。

*Ōno-kantoku no eiga ga zen'ei-**geijutsu** ka, tada no poruno ka to iu mondai o, eiga–hyōron-ka dake ni makaseyō to iu iken ni wa hantai desu.*

I don't go along with the view that we should leave it up to cinema critics to decide whether Director Ōno's films are of the avant-garde or are merely pornography.

　　＊ *zen'ei*: vanguard, avant-garde

22. 日本に亡命*しようとしていた北京の曲芸師は、諦めて帰国しましたが、これからどうなるでしょうか。

*Nihon ni bōmei shiyō to shite ita pekin no **kyokugei**-shi wa, akiramete kikoku shimashita ga, kore kara dō naru deshō ka.*

The Chinese acrobat who tried to seek asylum in Japan has given up and returned to China. I wonder what will become of him/her.

　　＊ *bōmei suru*: take refuge in another country; go into exile

23. クヌート・ティルバーグ氏は、数年前に宣教師として日本に来て偶然に芸能界と関係を作り、有名なタレントになりました。

*Kunūto-tirubāgu shi wa, sūnen-mae ni senkyō-shi to shite nihon ni kite gūzen ni **geinō-kai** to kankei o tsukuri, yūmei na tarento ni narimashita.*

Knut Tilberg came to Japan some years ago as a missionary, happened to get himself involved in the world of Japanese show business, and became quite a celebrity.

美術 *bijutsu* fine arts

絵画 (*kaiga*) painting, pictorial art

画法 (*gahō*) (art of) painting

絵 (*e*) (a) painting, drawing

油絵 (*abura-e*) (an) oil painting

水彩画 (*suisai-ga*) (a) watercolor painting

フレスコ画 (*furesuko-ga*) (a) fresco painting

日本画 (*nihon-ga*) (a) Japanese-style painting

墨絵 (*sumi-e*) (an) India (East Asian) ink painting

水墨画 (*suiboku-ga*) (same as above)

宗教画 (*shūkyō-ga*) religious painting

浮世絵 (*ukiyo-e*) ukiyo-e, color print

山水画 (*sansui-ga*) (a) landscape painting

肖像(画) (*shōzō[-ga]*) (a) portrait (painting)

壁画 (*hekiga*) (a) mural, mural/fresco painting

版画 (*hanga*) woodblock printing, (a) woodblock print

    版画家 (*hanga-ka*) woodblock printer

石版 (*sekiban/sekihan*) lithography

    石版画 (*sekiban-ga/sekihan-ga*) lithograph

彫刻 (*chōkoku*) sculpture, carving, engraving

塑像 (*sozō*) modeling

陶芸 (*tōgei*) ceramic arts (see above)

    陶器 (*tōki*) pottery

    磁器 (*jiki*) porcelain

    陶工 (*tōkō*) potter, ceramist

東洋美術 (*tōyō-bijutsu*) East Asian art

西洋美術 (*seiyō-bijutsu*) Western art

古典美術 (*koten-bijutsu*) classical art

中世美術 (*chūsei-bijutsu*) medieval art

現代美術 (*gendai-bijutsu*) modern/contemporary art

エジプト美術 (*ejiputo-bijutsu*) Egyptian art

ルネッサンス美術 (*runessansu-bijutsu*) Renaissance art

バロック式 (*barokku-shiki*) Baroque style

ゴシック式 (*goshikku-shiki*) Gothic style

ロマネスク式 (*romanesuku-shiki*) Romanesque style

新古典主義 (*shin–koten-shugi*) Neo-classicism

ロマンチシズム (*romanchishizumu*) Romanticism (cf. Ch. 1)

リアリズム (*riarizumu*) realism

モダニズム (*modanizumu*) modernism

印象派 (*inshō-ha*) impressionism (cf. Chapter 1)

後期印象派 (*kōki–inshō-ha*) Post-impressionism

キュービズム (*kyūbizumu*) Cubism, also 立体派 *rittai-ha*

シュールレアリズム (*shūru-rearizumu*) Surrealism

プリミティブアート (*purimitibu-āto*) primitive art

ポップアート (*poppu-āto*) pop art

具象美術 (*gushō-bijutsu*) representational art

抽象美術 (*chūshō-bijutsu*) abstract art

24. 日本の浮世絵は、ヨーロッパの印象派に大きな影響を与えました。

*Nihon no **ukiyo-e** wa, yōroppa no **inshō-ha** ni ōkina eikyō o atae-mashita.*

Japanese ukiyo-e had considerable influence on European impressionism.

25. 家族を養うために、新古典派のアングルは、18年間肖像画を描いていました。

*Kazoku o yashinau tame ni, **shin–koten-ha** no anguru wa, jūhachi-nenkan **shōzō-ga** o kaite imashita.*

The Neo-classical painter [Jean Auguste Dominique] Ingres painted portraits for eighteen years in order to support his family.

26. 「美術のことは何も分からないが、自分の好きな作品は分かる」とは、トルーマン米大統領の有名な発言です。

*"**Bijutsu** no koto wa nani mo wakaranai ga, jibun no suki na saku-hin wa wakaru" to wa, torūman bei-daitōryō no yūmei na hatsugen desu.*

"I don't know anything about art, but I know what I like" are the well-known words of US President Harry Truman.

音楽 *ongaku* Music

洋楽 (*yōgaku*) traditional Western music

邦楽 (*hōgaku*) traditional Japanese music

音楽理論 (*ongaku-riron*) musicology

旋律 (*senritsu*) melody (cf. メロディー *merodī*)

和声(法) (*wasei[-hō]*) harmony

コード (*kōdo*) chord

音階 (*onkai*) scale

音符 (*onpu*) note

全音符 (*zen-onpu*) whole note

半音符 (*han-onpu*) half note

四分音符 (*shibu-onpu*) quarter note

装飾音 (*sōshoku-on*) grace note

休止符 (*kyūshi-fu*) rest

全・半・四分 休止符 (*zen-/han-/shibu–kyūshi-fu*) whole/-half/quarter rest

テンポ (*tenpo*) tempo

律動 (*ritsudō*) rhythm (cf. リズム *rizumu*)

(長・短)調 (*[chō-/tan-]chō*) (major/minor) key

イロハニホヘト (*i-ro-ha-ni-ho-he-to*) A B C D E F G

嬰 (*ei*) sharp

変 (*hen*) flat

嬰ハ短調 (*ei-ha–tanchō*) C# minor

ト音譜表 (*to-on–fuhyō*) treble clef

低音部譜表 (*tei-onbu–fuhyō*) bass clef

ソプラノ (*sopurano*) soprano

アルト (*aruto*) alto

テノール/テナー (*tenōru/tenā*) tenor

バス (*basu*) bass

オーケストラ (*ōkesutora*) orchestra

木管楽器 (*mokkan-gakki*) woodwind instruments

金管楽器 (*kinkan-gakki*) brass wind instruments

絃楽器 (*gen-gakki*) string instruments

打楽器 (*da-gakki*) percussion instruments

Western Music *yōgaku* 洋楽

音楽会 (*ongakkai*) concert (cf. コンサート *konsāto*)

演奏 (*ensō*) performance [+ *suru*]

演奏会 (*ensō-kai*) a recital, concert

交響曲 (*kōkyō-kyoku*) symphony

管弦楽曲 (*kangen-gakkyoku*) orchestral music

協奏曲 (*kyōsō-kyoku*) concerto (also コンチェルト *konche-ruto*)

器楽曲 (*kigaku-kyoku*) instrumental music

室内楽曲 (*shitsunai-gakkyoku*) chamber music

歌劇 (*kageki*) lyric drama, opera

オペラ (*opera*) opera

ソナタ (*sonata*) sonata

バロック音楽 (*barokku-ongaku*) Baroque music

古典派音楽 (*koten-ha–ongaku*) Classical music

ロマン派音楽 (*roman-ha–ongaku*) Romantic music

現代音楽 (*gendai-ongaku*) modern music

ジャズ (*jazu*) jazz

ロック (*rokku*) rock

Japanese Music *hōgaku* 邦楽

神楽 (*kagura*) Shinto music and dancing

雅楽 (*gagaku*) court music

舞楽 (*bugaku*) court music and dance

琵琶 (*biwa*) biwa, Japanese lute

琴 (*koto*) koto, Japanese zither

三味線 (*shamisen*) shamisen, plucked lute

尺八 (*shakuhachi*) shakuhachi, bamboo flute

鼓 (*tsuzumi*) hand-drum

太鼓 (*taiko*) drum

鈴 (*suzu*) bell

鐘 (*shō*) (Chinese) gong

囃子 (*hayashi*) percussion and flute ensemble

27. ショパンの嬰ハ短調幻想曲は、日本でよく演奏されます。

*Shopan no **ei-ha-tanchō**–gensō-kyoku wa, nihon de yoku ensō sare-masu.*

Chopin's "Fantasy in C# minor" is often performed in Japan.

28. ベートーベンの交響曲の中で、一番好きなのはどれですか。

*Bētōben no **kōkyō-kyoku** no naka de, ichiban suki na no wa dore desu ka.*

Which is your favorite Beethoven symphony?

29. 日本の音楽史の専門家ヴェルネル・ビーレフェルト氏は、流行歌を中心とする大正時代の音楽について、おもしろそうな本を書きました。

*Nihon no ongaku-shi no senmon-ka veruneru-bīreferuto-shi wa, **ryūkō-ka** o chūshin to suru taishō jidai no ongaku ni tsuite, omoshirosō na hon o kakimashita.*

Werner Bielefeld, a specialist in the history of Japanese music, has written what seems to be an interesting book about Taisho-era music, centering on popular songs.

文学 *bungaku* Literature
演芸学 *engei-gaku* Performing Arts

General

世界文学 (*sekai-bungaku*) world literature

散文 (*sanbun*) prose (lit. scattered writing)

創作 (*sōsaku*) fiction

小説 (*shōsetsu*) novel (cf. Chapter 1)

短編小説 (*tanpen-shōsetsu*) short story

ノンフィクション (*non-fikushon*) nonfiction

韻文 (*inbun*) verse (lit. rhyme writing)

叙情詩 (*jojō-shi*) lyric poetry (lit. description-feeling poetry)

叙事詩 (*joji-shi*) epic poetry (lit. description-thing poetry)

(演)劇 (*[en]geki*) drama

悲劇 (*higeki*) tragedy (lit. sad drama)

喜劇 (*kigeki*) comedy (lit. joyful drama)

Japanese

国文学 (*kokubun-gaku*) Japanese literature (as an academic subject)

物語 (*monogatari*) tale

小説 (*shōsetsu*) novel

随筆 (*zuihitsu*) essay (lit. follow-the-pen)

短歌 (*tanka*) 31-syllable Japanese poem (lit. short poem)

狂歌 (*kyōka*) comic tanka

和歌 (*waka*) same as *tanka* (lit. Japanese poem)

俳句 (*haiku*) haiku (17-syllable Japanese poem" [5-7-5])

川柳 (*senryū*) satirical haiku

能 (*nō*) Noh (drama)

歌舞伎 (*kabuki*) Kabuki

狂言 (*kyōgen*) interact, comedy, Noh farce (lit. mad words)

文楽 (*bunraku*) Bunraku, puppet theater

30. 紫式部が『源氏物語』を完成したのは、11世紀の初め頃でした。

*Murasaki shikibu ga "Genji **monogatari**" o kansei shita no wa, jūisseiki no hajime-goro deshita.*

Murasaki Shikibu completed *The Tale of Genji* at the beginning of the eleventh century.

31. 日本の若者は、世界文学も日本文学もあまり読まないかもしれませんが、夏目漱石の『坊ちゃん』や『こころ』ぐらいならだ

れでも知っているでしょう。

*Nihon no wakamono wa, **sekai-bungaku** mo **nihon-bungaku** mo amari yomanai kamo shiremasen ga, natsume sōseki no "botchan" ya "kokoro" gurai nara dare de mo shitte iru deshō.*

Japanese young people may read very little world literature or Japanese literature, but virtually anyone will know Sōseki Natsume's *Botchan* or *Kokoro*.

32. シェークスピアは、オリビエの『リチャード三世』の演出を見たらどんな反応を示すでしょうか。

*Shēkusupia wa, oribie no "richādo-sansei" no **enshutsu** o mitara donna hannō o shimesu deshō ka.*

How would Shakespeare react if he saw Olivier's interpretation of *Richard III*?

言語学 (*gengo-gaku*) Linguistics

語学 (*gogaku*) language study

英語学 (*eigo-gaku*) English language and linguistics

国語学 (*kokugo-gaku*) (traditional) Japanese linguistics

音声学 (*onsei-gaku*) phonetics (the study of the production and perception of speech sounds)

母音 (*boin*) vowel (lit. mother sound)

子音 (*shi'in*) consonant (lit. child sound)

閉鎖音 (*heisa-on*) stop (e.g., p, t, k, b, d, g)

破裂音 (*haretsu-on*) plosive (same as above)

摩擦音 (*masatsu-on*) fricative (e.g., f, s, sh, h, z)

破擦音 (*hasatsu-on*) affricate (e.g., ch, ts, dz)

流音 (*ryūon*) liquid (e.g., l, r)

鼻音 (*bion*) nasal (e.g., m, n, ng)

音韻学 (*on'in-gaku*) phonology (the study of sound sytems, also 音韻論 *on'in-ron*)

音韻 (*on'in*) phoneme (e.g., ん /n/, the syllabic nasal)

音韻組織 (*on'in-soshiki*) sound system

異音 (*ion*) allophone (e.g., /N/ → [m], [n], [ng] ...)

同化 (*dōka*) assimilation (e.g., 新聞 *shimbun* "newspaper" vs. 新婚 *shingkon* "newly-wed")

異化 (*ika*) dissimilation (e.g., Latin *marmor* > English marble)

削除 (*sakujo*) deletion (e.g., know > [no:])

語中音挿入 (*gochū-on–sōnyū*) epenthesis (e.g., 山王 *san + ō* → *sannō*)

剰音 (*jō'on*) excrescent sound (e.g., coat → *kōto*)

語頭音添加 (*gotō'on-tenka*) prothesis (addition of an initial sound, e.g., Latin *scutum* "shield" > Spanish *escudo*)

音韻転換 (*on'in-tenkan*) metathesis (lit. sound position switch, e.g., 新た *arata* vs. 新しい *atarashii* "new")

形態学 (*keitai-gaku*) morphology (the study of word and phrase structure; also 形態論 *keitai-ron*)

動詞活用 (*dōshi-katsuyō*) verb conjugation

格変化 (*kaku-henka*) case inflection

屈折言語 (*kussetsu-gengo*) inflecting language

膠着言語 (*kōchaku-gengo*) agglutinating language

孤立言語 (*koritsu-gengo*) isolating language

統語学 (*tōgo-gaku*) syntax (the study of phrase and sentence structure; also 統語論 *tōgo-ron*)

主語 (*shugo*) subject

述語 (*jutsugo*) predicate

名詞 (*meishi*) noun

代名詞 (*dai-meishi*) pronoun

動詞 (*dōshi*) verb

助動詞 (*jo-dōshi*) auxiliary verb

形容詞 (*keiyō-shi*) adjective

副詞 (*fukushi*) adverb

前置詞 (*zenchi-shi*) preposition

接続詞 (*setsuzoku-shi*) conjunction

感嘆詞 (*kantan-shi*) interjection

造語法 (*zōgo-hō*) word formation

接頭語 (*settō-go*) prefix

接尾語 (*setsubi-go*) suffix

語彙論 (*goi-ron*) lexicology

大和言葉 (*yamato-kotoba*) native Japanese

漢語 (*kango*) Sino-Japanese (Chinese loanwords usually written in kanji)

外来語 (*gairai-go*) foreign words (in reference to Japanese, usually non-Chinese)

翻訳借用 (*hon'yaku-shakuyō*) loan-translation (e.g., the word 核家族 *kaku-kazoku*, translated from the English "nuclear family")

意味論 (*imi-ron*) semantics (lit. meaning theory)

比喩 (*hiyu*) simile, metaphor

直喩 (*chokuyu*) simile (lit. direct figure of speech)

隠喩 (*in'yu*) metaphor (lit. hidden figure of speech)

誇張 (*kochō*) hyperbole

婉曲表現 (*enkyoku hyōgen*) euphemism

タブー語 (*tabū-go*) taboo word

差別語 (*sabetsu-go*) discriminatory language

Traditional Japanese linguistic terminology

国語学 (*kokugo-gaku*) national language study

音便 (*onbin*) euphony, contraction, e.g., *kikite* > *kiite* "listening"; *sumite* > *sunde* "living"; *nemurite* > *nemutte* "sleeping"

助詞 (*joshi*) (postpositional) particle, e.g., *wa, ga, ni, o, no,* etc. (also known as てにをは *te ni o ha*, four representative examples)

形容動詞 (*keiyō-dōshi*) nominal adjective (lit. adjectival verb), e.g., きれいな絵 (*kirei na e*) beautiful picture

活用 (*katsuyō*) conjugation (of verbs and adjectives)

未然形 (*mizen-kei*) imperfective (e.g., **kuwanai** "does not eat")

連用形 (*ren'yō-kei*) conjunctive (e.g., **kuitai** "wants to eat")

終止形 (*shūshi-kei*) predicative (e.g., **kuu** "eats")

連体形 (*rentai-kei*) attributive (e.g., **kuu** *hito* "eating person")

仮定形 (*katei-kei*) hypothetical (e.g., **kueba** "if … eats")

命令形 (*meirei-kei*) imperative (e.g., **kue** "eat!")

In classical Japanese, the form represented by **kue-** is treated as 已然形 *izen-kei* "perfective"; **kueba**, for example, means "having eaten."

33. 中国語と日本語は同じ語族に属していないし、音韻組織と文法構造から見ても、著しく差異*のある言語です。

Chūgoku-go to nihon-go wa onaji gozoku ni zoku-shite inai shi, **on'in**-*soshiki to bunpō-kōzō kara mite mo, ichijirushiku sai no aru gengo desu.*

Chinese and Japanese do not belong to the same language family, and are also strikingly different in regard to sound system and grammar.

* *sai*; difference, a difference

34. 大学紛争時代の1969年にサンフランシスコ州立カレッジの学長になったS.I. ハヤカワ氏は、すでに意味論者として知られていました。

*Daigaku-funsō–jidai no sen-kyūhyaku-rokujūkyū-nen ni sanfuran-shisuko-shūritsu-karejji no gakuchō ni natta S. I. Hayakawa-shi wa, sude ni **imi-ron**sha to shite shirarete imashita.*

When S. I. Hayakawa became president of San Francisco State College at the time of the campus upheavals of 1969, he was already known as a semanticist.

35. 古代日本語の動詞活用には、終止形と連体形が異なる[＊]場合があります。例えば、現代日本語の「紅葉が落ちる」と「落ちる紅葉」とは、「紅葉落つ」と「落つる紅葉」になります。

*Kodai–nihon-go no **dōshi-katsuyō** ni wa, **shūshi-kei** to **rentai-kei** ga kotonaru baai ga arimasu. Tatoeba, gendai–nihon-go no "momiji ga ochiru" to "ochiru momiji" to wa, "momiji otsu" to "otsuru momiji" ni narimasu.*

In the verb conjugations of Old Japanese, the predicative and the attributive are sometimes different in form. For example, the forms corresponding to Modern Japanese *momiji ga ochiru* [autumn leaves fall] and *ochiru momiji* [falling autumn leaves] are *momiji otsu* and *otsuru momiji*.

＊ *kotonaru*: to be different

歴史学 *rekishi-gaku* History

General

史料編纂 (*shiryō-hensan*) historiography
歴史主義 (*rekishi-shugi*) historicism, historical relativism
史的唯物論 (*shiteki–yuibutsu-ron*) historical materialism (Marxist)

時代 (*jidai*) age, era
　旧石器時代 (*kyū–sekki-jidai*) palaeolithic age (Old Stone Age)
　新石器時代 (*shin–sekki-jidai*) neolithic age (New Stone Age)
　青銅器時代 (*seidōki–jidai*) Bronze Age
　鉄器時代 (*tekki-jidai*) Iron Age

　古代 (*kodai*) ancient (times)
　中世 (*chūsei*) mediaeval (times)
　近代 (*kindai*) modern (times)
　現代 (*gendai*) contemporary (times)

文明 (*bunmei*) civilization
文化 (*bunka*) culture
帝国 (*teikoku*) empire

王朝 (*ōchō*) dynasty

ローマ法王 (*rōma-hō'ō*) Roman Pontiff, pope (also 教皇 *kyōkō*)

(国)王 (*[koku]ō*) "monarch" / 女王 (*jo'ō*) queen

封建制度 (*hōken-seido*) feudalism (feudal system)

貴族 (*kizoku*) aristocracy

    公爵 (*kōshaku*) duke

    侯爵 (*kōshaku*) marquess

    伯爵 (*hakushaku*) earl, count

    子爵 (*shishaku*) viscount

    男爵 (*danshaku*) lord, baron

Japanese

縄文時代 (*jōmon-jidai*) Jomon period (10,000 B.C.–300 B.C.)

弥生時代 (*yayoi-jidai*) Yayoi period (300 B.C.–A.D. 300)

大和時代 (*yamato-jidai*) Yamato period (300–550)

飛鳥時代 (*asuka-jidai*) Asuka period (550–710)

奈良時代 (*nara-jidai*) Nara period (710–794)

平安時代 (*heian-jidai*) Heian period (794–1185)

鎌倉時代 (*kamakura-jidai*) Kamakura period (1185–1333)

室町時代 (*muromachi-jidai*) Muromachi period (1333–1568)

    足利時代 (*ashikaga-jidai*) Ashikaga period (same as above)

安土桃山時代 (*azuchi-momoyama–jidai*) Azuchi-Momoyama period (1558–1600)

江戸時代 (*edo-jidai*) Edo period (1600–1868)

徳川時代 (*tokugawa-jidai*) Tokugawa period (same as above)

明治時代 (*meiji-jidai*) Meiji period (1868–1912)

大正時代 (*taishō-jidai*) Taisho period (1912–26)

昭和時代 (*shōwa-jidai*) Showa period (1926–89)

平成時代 (*heisei-jidai*) Heisei period (1989–present)

天皇 (*tennō*) Japanese emperor

将軍 (*shōgun*) shogun

幕府 (*bakufu*) shogunate (lit. tent government)

士農工商 (*shi-nō-kō-shō*) warriors, farmers, artisans, tradesmen (the four hierarchical classes under the Tokugawa shogunate)

明治維新 (*meiji-ishin*) Meiji Restoration

大正デモクラシー (*taishō-demokurashī*) Taisho Democracy

軍国主義 (*gunkoku-shugi*) militarism
太平洋戦争 (*taiheiyō-sensō*) the Pacific War
占領時代 (*senryō-jidai*) the Occupation
戦後時代 (*sengo-jidai*) postwar period

36. 日本における歴史学研究は、まだマルクス主義の独断的な決定
論の影響を被って*います。

*Nihon ni okeru **rekishi-gaku**–kenkyū wa, mada marukusu-shugi no
dokudan-teki na kettei-ron no eikyō o kōmutte imasu.*

Historical research in Japan is still suffering from the dogmatic
determinism of Marxism.

* *eikyō o kōmuru*: be subject to, or come under, the influence of

37. 中央ヨーロッパの鉄器時代は、日本の鉄器時代よりも1000年ほ
ど前のことです。

*Chūō-yōroppa no **tekki-jidai** wa, nihon no tekki-jidai yori mo sen-
nen hodo mae no koto desu.*

Central Europe's Iron Age predates Japan's by a millennium.

38. 「ショウグン」という小説と映画のせいか、封建時代の日本を
誤解したり、昔と今の日本を混同したり*する欧米人が多いよ
うです。

*"Shōgun" to iu shōsetsu to eiga no sei ka, **hōken-jidai** no nihon o
gokai shitari, mukashi to ima no nihon o kondō shitari suru
ōbei-jin ga ōi yō desu.*

There seem to be many Europeans and Americans who, perhaps
because of the novel and film *Shogun*, misunderstand Japan's
feudal period or confuse the Japan of long ago with the Japan
of today.

* *kondō suru*: to treat two separate things as one and the same; mistake one thing for
another

社会学 *shakai-gaku* Sociology

社会組織 (*shakai-soshiki*) social organization
社会秩序 (*shakai-chitsujo*) social order
社会事情 (*shakai-jijō*) social conditions
社会生活 (*shakai-seikatsu*) social life
集団生活 (*shūdan-seikatsu*) life in a group
個人生活 (*kojin-seikatsu*) life as an individual
集団心理 (*shūdan-shinri*) group psychology
社会運動 (*shakai-undō*) social movement
大衆 (*taishū*) mass(es)
大衆運動 (*taishū-undō*) mass movement
社会的総数 (*shaka-teki*–*sōsū*) social aggregates

人口 (*jinkō*) population
人種 (*jinshu*) race
民族的集団 (*minzoku-teki–shūdan*) ethnic group
宗教 (*shūkyō*) religion
年齢 (*nenrei*) age
職業 (*shokugyō*) occupation
教育 (*kyōiku*) education
収入 (*shūnyū*) income

階級 (*kaikyū*) social classes
　上流階級 (*jōryū-kaikyū*) upper class
　中流の上層階級 (*chūryū no jōsō-kaikyū*) upper middle class
　中流階級 (*chūryū-kaikyū*) middle class
　中流の下層階級 (*chūryū no kasō-kaikyū*) lower middle class
　下層階級 (*kasō-kaikyū*) lower class, underclass

知識階級 (*chishiki-kaikyū*) the educated classes
特権階級 (*tokken-kaikyū*) the privileged classes
有産階級 (*yūsan-kaikyū*) property-owning classes
無産階級 (*musan-kaikyū*) propertyless classes, proletariat
労働階級 (*rōdō-kaikyū*) working classes

階級意識 (*kaikyū-ishiki*) class consciousness
階級闘争 (*kaikyū-tōsō*) class warfare (Marxist)

民族 (*minzoku*) ethnos, people
　民族意識 (*minzoku-ishiki*) ethnic identity
　少数民族 (*shōsū-minzoku*) ethnic minority
　多民族国家 (*ta-minzoku–kokka*) multiethnic state
　単一民族国家 (*tan'itsu-minzoku–kokka*) ethnically homogeneous state

開かれた社会 (*hirakareta shakai*) open society
閉鎖(的)社会 (*heisa[-teki]-shakai*) closed society

人種(的)差別 (*jinshu(-teki)-sabetsu*) racial discrimination
疎外(感) (*sogai[-kan]*) (sense of) alienation
社会的連帯 (*shakai-teki–rentai*) social solidarity

アルコール依存症 (*arukōru–izon-shō*) alcoholism
麻薬常習 (*mayaku-jōshū*) drug addiction

拡大家族 (*kakudai-kazoku*) extended family

核家族 (*kaku-kazoku*) nuclear family

内縁関係 (*naien-kankei*) common-law marriage

離婚 (*rikon*) divorce

再婚 (*saikon*) remarriage

私生児出産 (*shisei-ji–shussan*) illegitimate birth

未婚の母 (*mikon no haha*) unwed mother

風俗紊乱 (*fūzoku-binran*) offense against public morals

乱交 (*rankō*) promiscuous sexual relations

性欲倒錯 (*seiyoku-tōsaku*) sexual perversion

近親相姦 (*kinshin-sōkan*) incest

同性愛 (*dōsei-ai*) homosexuality

世論調査 (*yoron-chōsa*) public opinion poll

人口動態統計 (*jinkō-dōtai–tōkei*) vital statistics

人口学 (*jinkō-gaku*) demography

39. 19世紀に社会学の発展を主導したエミール・デュルケームの一
番有名な作品では、「自殺」を取り扱っています。

*Jūkyū-seiki ni **shakai-gaku** no hatten o shudō shita emīru-dyuru-
kēmu no ichiban yūmei na sakuhin de wa, "jisatsu" o tori-
atsukatte imasu.*

In the best known work of Emile Durkheim, who led the development of sociology in the nineteenth century, the subject of suicide is treated.

40. 「中流社会」や「単一民族」としての日本のイメージがどれほ
ど現実であるかは、まだ議論の決着がついて*いません。

*"**Chūryū**-shakai" ya "**tan'itsu-minzoku**" to shite no nihon no imēji
ga dore hodo genjitsu de aru ka wa, mada giron no ketchaku ga
tsuite imasen.*

The debate continues on how much the image of Japan as a "mid-
dle-class, ethnically homogeneous society" is a reality.

   * *ketchaku ga tsuku*: come to a conclusion, an end; be settled

41. 欧米と違って、日本の社会で核家族が顕著*になったのは最近
のことです。

*Ōbei to chigatte, nihon no shakai de **kaku-kazoku** ga kencho ni
natta no wa saikin no koto desu.*

In contrast to Europe and America, it is only recently that the nuclear family has become prominent in Japan.

   * *kencho*: conspicuous, striking, remarkable

CHAPTER

V

Science and Technology

In Western European languages, words for "science," including the English term, originally referred to knowledge in general, cf. German *Wissenschaft* (< *wissen* "know"). When J. G. Fichte published his *Wissenschaftslehre* in 1794, for example, his concern was the "theory (study) of knowledge," and his work is thus literally translated into Japanese as 知識学 *chishiki-gaku*.

Nevertheless, when Meiji-era Japanese scholars looked for a term to represent the more specific meaning the word *Wissenschaft* has in our own day, they settled on 科学 *kagaku*, lit. "section study." The appropriateness of the choice may not be apparent until we remember that acquiring knowledge or understanding is, in part, a process of dividing and sorting, as is reflected in the native Japanese word 分かる *wakaru*. Though translated as "know, understand," it literally means "(be) divide (d)," cf. (transitive) 分ける *wakeru* "divide." Not coincidentally, *scientia* (< *scire* "know") itself derives from Indo-European **skei-* "cut, divide, separate," which yields schedule (cf. Japanese 時間割 *jikan-wari*, lit. time-breakup) and *schism*, *shed*, *sheath*, and even the vulgar English word for excrement.

In this chapter, we continue to look at the world of learning, this time focusing on the realm of 科学 *kagaku*. We begin with a summary of the major fields in the natural sciences, some of which are also found in the previous chapter. We then continue with examples and illustrations of terms which specialist and layman alike can expect to encounter.

Science
科学 KAGAKU

The 理学部 *rigaku-bu* "faculty (college) of science" in a Japanese university includes both the "hard sciences" and mathematics. At one institution, we find the following departments and sections:

数学科 (*sūgakka*) mathematics department
    代数学 (*daisū-gaku*) algebra
    幾何学 (*kika-gaku*) geometry
    応用数学 (*ōyō-sūgaku*) applied mathematics
    統計数学 (*tōkei-sūgaku*) statistics

物理学科 (*butsuri-gakka*) physics department
    理論物理学 (*riron–butsuri-gaku*) theoretical physics
    原子物理学 (*genshi–butsuri-gaku*) atomic physics
    物性物理学 (*bussei–butsuri-gaku*) solid state physics
    実験物理学 (*jikken–butsuri-gaku*) experimental physics

化学科 (*kagakka*) chemistry department
    物理化学 (*butsuri-kagaku*) physical chemistry
    無機化学 (*muki-kagaku*) inorganic chemistry
    有機化学 (*yūki-kagaku*) organic chemistry
    生化学 (*sei-kagaku*) biochemistry

生物学科 (*seibutsu-gakka*) biology department
    形態学 (*keitai-gaku*) morphology (also a term in linguistics)
    生理学 (*seiri-gaku*) physiology
    生態学 (*seitai-gaku*) ecology
    系統学 (*keitō-gaku*) systematics

地学科 (*chigakka*) earth sciences department
    地質学 (*chishitsu-gaku*) geology
    鉱物学 (*kōbutsu-gaku*) minerology

Needless to say, the list is hardly exhaustive. Conspicuously missing, for example, is the entire field of 天文学 *tenmon-gaku* "astronomy." Of other subjects that readily come to mind, we might mention the following ten:

三角法 (*sankaku-hō*) trigonometry
微分積分学 (*bibun–sekibun-gaku*) differential and integral calculus
天体物理学 (*tentai–butsuri-gaku*) astrophysics

微視物理学 (*bishi–butsuri-gaku*) microphysics (also ミクロ物
理学 *mikuro–butsuri-gaku*)

植物学 (*shokubutsu-gaku*) botany

動物学 (*dōbutsu-gaku*) zoology

古生物学 (*koseibutsu-gaku*) paleontology

自然人類学 (*shizen–jinrui-gaku*) physical anthropology

気象学 (*kishō-gaku*) meteorology

海洋学 (*kaiyō-gaku*) oceanography

1. 健次君は、代数方程式*を解くのは上手ですが、立体†幾何学は
どうしてもできません。

*Kenji-kun wa, **daisū**–hōtei-shiki o toku no wa jōzu desu ga, rittai–
kika-gaku wa dōshite mo dekimasen.*

Kenji is good at solving algebraic equations, but he cannot for the
life of him do solid geometry.

※ *hōtei-shiki*: equation
† *rittai*: cubic, three dimensions, solid

2. ハンブルク大学で経営経済学を勉強していた時、一番苦しかっ
たのはやはり統計（数）学でした。

*Hanburuku-daigaku de keiei–keizai-gaku o benkyō shite ita toki,
ichiban kurushikatta no wa yahari **tōkei-(sū)gaku** deshita.*

When I was studying business economics at the University of
Hamburg, the greatest ordeal was, after all, statistics.

Even if quadratic equations (二次方程式 *niji–hōtei-shiki*) are
not your cup of tea, you will need to know the basic terms for
ordinary arithmetic (算数 *sansū*):

足す (*tasu*) add (足し算 *tashizan* "addition")

引く (*hiku*) subtract (引き算 *hikizan* "subtraction")

掛ける (*kakeru*) multiply (掛け算 *kakezan* "multiplication")

割る (*waru*) divide (割算 *warizan* "division")

3. 10＋5は15になる。83－17は66になる。12×9は108になる。22÷
4は5.5になる。

*Jū tasu go wa jūgo ni naru. Hachijū-san hiku jūnana wa rokujū-
roku ni naru. Jūni kakeru kyū wa hyakuhachi ni naru. Nijū-ni
waru yon wa go-ten-go* [the vowel of the first *go* elongated] *ni
naru.*

$10 + 5 = 15.$ $83 - 17 = 66.$ $12 \times 9 = 108.$ $22 \div 4 - 5.5.$

Two words for "ratio," one native Japanese, the other Sino-
Japanese, are 割合 *wariai* and 比率 *hiritsu*.

4. 北アイルランドのプロテスタント信者は、カトリック信者に対

して２対１の割合（比率）です。

*Kita-airurando no purotesutanto-shinja wa, katorikku-shinja ni taishite ni tai ichi no **wariai (hiritsu)** desu.*

The ratio of Protestants to Catholics in Northern Ireland is two to one.

割 *wari* is used by itself in the sense of "share, rate, ratio," cf. (Sino-Japanese) 率 *ritsu*:

5. 鈴子さんは、一週間50万円の割でお父さんの遺産を全部使ってしまいました。

*Suzuko-san wa, isshūkan gojū-man-en no **wari** de otōsan no isan o zenbu tsukatte shimaimashita.*

Suzuko squandered all the money she inherited from her father at the rate of ¥500,000 a week.

As a unit of measurement, *wari* means 10%, in contrast to 分 *bu* 1%.

6. 死刑の廃止運動を支持している日本人は、まだ3割5分にもなっていないそうです。

*Shikei no haishi-undō o shiji-shite iru nihon-jin wa, mada san-**wari** go-**bu** ni mo natte inai sō desu.*

The number of Japanese supporting the movement to abolish capital punishment reportedly still stands at less than 35%.

Fractions (分数 *bunsū*) are expressed in English as numerator/denominator (分子・分母 *bunshi-bunbo*); in Japanese, the order is reversed, so that instead of "two-thirds," one says 3分の2 *sanbun no ni*, i.e., "of three parts, two." The word for "percent" is borrowed from English as パーセント *pāsento* (e.g., 32 パーセント *sanjū-ni pāsento* 32%).

7. 今日の新聞によると、ボルチモア市民の3分の1は、機能的非識字者だそうです。

Kyō no shinbun ni yoru to, boruchimoa-shimin no san-bun no ichi wa, kinō-teki–hi-shikiji-sha da sō desu.

According to today's newspaper, one-third of Baltimore's citizens are functional illiterates.

8. アメリカにおける1990年の私生児率は26％に上がりました。

*Amerika ni okeru sen-kyūhyaku-kyūjū-nen no shisei-ji–ritsu wa nijūroku-**pāsento** ni agarimashita.*

In 1990 the rate of illegitimate births in America rose to 26%.

9. 「物体✽の運動量†は、その質量◆と速度✿の積✚である」というのは、ニュートン物理学の中心的な原則です。

"Buttai no undō-ryō wa, sono shitsuryō to sokudo no seki de aru"
*to iu no wa, nyūton–**butsuri-gaku** no chūshin-teki na gensoku*
desu.

That "the momentum of an object is the product of its mass and its
velocity" is a central principle of Newtonian physics.

❋ *buttai*: physical object
† *undō-ryō*: momentum
❖ *shitsuryō*: mass
✿ *sokudo*: velocity
✚ *seki*: product

10. 原子物理学と言いますと、私が知っているのは子供の時に習っ
た「陽子」・「中性子」・「電子」のことだけです。

***Genshi–butsuri-gaku** to iimasu to, watashi ga shitte iru no wa
kodomo no toki ni naratta "yōshi," "chūsei-shi," "denshi" no
koto dake desu.*

If you mention atomic physics, all I know is what I learnt when I
was small about protons, neutrons, and electrons.

11. 水の3分の2は水素❋、3分の1は酸素†です。
*Mizu no san**bun** no ni wa suiso, san**bun** no ichi wa sanso desu.*

Water consists of two parts hydrogen and one part oxygen.

❋ *suiso*: hydrogen
† *sanso*: oxygen

12. 地球のほとんどの生物は酸素を頼りに生きていますが、体積❋
で空気の5分の4ほどを占めているのは窒素†です。

*Chikyū no hotondo no seibutsu wa sanso o tayori ni ikite imasu ga,
taiseki de kūki no go**bun** no yon hodo o shimete iru no wa chisso desu.*

Most life forms on earth depend on oxygen, but four-fifths of the
atmosphere consists of nitrogen.

❋ *taiseki*: volume
† *chisso*: nitrogen

13. 山田君は熱心な微生物学者❋だけど、全く単細胞❋的な人で、結
婚のことを全然考えていないらしい。一体人間の繁殖†する方
法を知っているのかしら。

*Yamada-kun wa nesshin na **bi-seibutsu-gaku**sha da kedo, mattaku
tansaibō-teki na hito de, kekkon no koto o zenzen kangaete inai
rashii. Ittai ningen no hanshoku suru hōhō o shitte iru no
kashira.*

Yamada may be a devoted microbiologist, but he's totally one-
sided (lit. single-celled) and apparently doesn't give a thought
to getting married. I wonder whether he even knows how human beings reproduce.

❋ *tan-saibo*: single cell
† *hanshoku*: breeding

14. 生態学者ではありませんが、露天採鉱❋による土壌浸食†がまだ

大きい問題になっているかどうか知りたいと思います。

***Seitai-gaku**sha de wa arimasen ga, roten-saikō ni yoru dojō-shin-shoku ga mada ōkii mondai ni natte iru ka dō ka shiritai to omoimasu.*

Even though I'm not an ecologist, I should like to know whether soil erosion caused by strip-mining is still a big problem.

 ＊ *roten-saikō*: strip-mining
 † *dojō-shinshoku*: soil erosion

15. 鉱物学者の橋本先生は、天然資源＊の豊富†なロシア共和国に深い興味をもっています。

***Kōbutsu-gaku**sha no hashimoto-sensei wa, tennen-shigen no hōfu na roshia–kyōwa-koku ni fukai kyōmi o motte imasu.*

Professor Hashimoto, a minerologist, has a deep interest in the Russian Republic with its wealth of natural resources.

 ＊ *tennen-shigen*: natural resources
 † *hōfu*: rich

Much of the task of science, true to the etymology of its name, consists of sorting and categorizing. Some important word elements to be mentioned in that regard are:

界 (*kai*) realm
門 (*mon*) phylum
網 (*mō*) class
目 (*moku*) order
科 (*ka*) family
属 (*zoku*) genus
種 (*shu*) species

 類 (*rui*) a cover term for class and order (cf. 種類 *shurui* "kind. variety")
 族 (*zoku*) family, group

16. 魚類や爬虫類などの動物は変温であり、鳥類と哺乳類は定温動物です。

*Gyo**rui** ya hachū-**rui** nado no dōbutsu wa hen'on de ari, chō**rui** to honyū-**rui** wa teion-dōbutsu desu.*

Coldblooded animals include fish and reptiles; birds and mammals are warmblooded.

17. 家の猫がネコ科ネコ属に属していることは知っていますが、何種かは分かりません。

*Uchi no neko ga neko-**ka** neko-**zoku** ni zoku-shite iru koto wa shitte imasu ga, nani-**shu** ka wa wakarimasen.*

I know that our cat belongs to the cat genus (*felis catus*) of the Felidae family, but I don't know its species.

Note that 属 *zoku* "genus" should not be confused with 族 "tribe, group," which is used to refer to chemical groups, e.g., 白金族 *hakkin-zoku* "platinum group."

Knowing the preference among English-speaking scientists for the Latin names given to families and genera, one might expect the Japanese names to use Sino-Japanese terminology. In fact, as can be seen here, ordinary native words predominate, though they are written in *katakana*, cf. イヌ科 *inu-ka* "Canidae."

18. イヌ科には、犬、狼、狐なども含まれています。

Inu-ka ni wa, inu, ōkami, kitsune nado mo fukumarete imasu.

The canine family [Canidae] includes dogs, wolves, and foxes.

19. 岩石は、火成岩、水成岩、変成岩という３つの種類に分かれています。例えば、軽石*は火成岩、粘板岩は水成岩、金剛石（ダイヤモンド）は変成岩です。

Ganseki wa, kasei-gan, suisei-gan, hensei-gan to iu mittsu no shurui ni wakete imasu. Tatoeba, karuishi wa kasei-gan, nenban-gan wa suisei-gan, kongō-seki (daiyamondo) wa hensei-gan desu.

We divide rocks into three categories: igneous (volcanic), aqueous (sedimentary), and metamorphic. Pumice is an example of igneous rock, slate of aqueous rock, and diamonds of metamorphic rock.

* *karuishi*: pumice (lit. light stone)

20. 植物界か動物界か分類するのが難しい生物もある。

Shokubutsu-kai ka dōbutsu-kai ka bunrui suru no ga muzukashii seibutsu mo aru.

Some organisms do not fall neatly into the categories of vegetable kingdom and animal kingdom.

21. 子供の時から軽石や黒曜石に興味を持っていたライトさんが地質学者になったのは、不思議ではない。

Kodomo no toki kara karuishi ya kokuyō-seki ni kyōmi o motte ita raito-san ga chishitsu-gakusha ni natta no wa, fushigi de wa nai.

Not surprisingly, Miss Wright, who was interested in pumice and obsidian from the time she was a child, has become a geologist.

If we look beyond earth and its resources to the solar system (太陽系 *taiyō-kei*) and interstellar space (星間空間 *seikan-kūkan*), we shall need at least a rudimentary lexical knowledge of the heavenly bodies, beginning with the planets (惑星 *waku-sei*, lit. fluctuating star). Their Sino-Japanese names are easy to remember. Those of the inner five, Mercury, Venus, Mars, Jupiter, and Saturn, are based on East Asia's five traditional elements—wood, fire, earth (soil), gold, and water—and thus correspond to names of the days of the week. (Students of Romance languages will know that Tuesday, Wednesday, Thursday, and Friday correspond to "Mars-day," "Mercury-day," "Jupiter-day," and "Venus-day." English Saturday likewise originally referred to "Saturn's Day.") The Sino-Japanese names for Neptune, Uranus, and Pluto reflect Greco-Roman mythology.

水星 (*suisei*) Mercury (lit. water star)

金星 (*kinsei*) Venus (lit. gold star)

火星 (*kasei*) Mars (lit. fire star)

木星 (*mokusei*) Jupiter (lit. wood star)

土星 (*dosei*) Saturn (lit. earth star)

天王星 (*ten'ō-sei*) Uranus (lit. heavenly king star)
海王星 (*kaiō-sei*) Neptune (lit. sea-king star)
冥王星 (*meiō-sei*) Pluto (lit. Hades-king star)

The Japanese term for asteroids or planetoids is simply 小惑星 *shōwaku-sei*, lit. "small planets."

Earth's moon is, of course, 月 *tsuki*, commonly referred to affectionately as お月様 *otsuki-sama* "Mr. Moon," but the moons of other planets are called 衛星 *eisei* "satellites," cf. 人工衛星 *jinkō-eisei* "artificial satellite," 通信衛星 *tsūshin-eisei* "telecommunications satellite."

There are three words for "sun" or "solar": native Japanese 日 *hi* (or お日様 *ohi-sama* "Mr. Sun"), as in 日焼け *hi-yake* "sunburn," and Sino-Japanese 太陽 *taiyō* and 日 *nichi-*. The latter appears in such compounds as 日曜日 *nichiyō-bi* "Sunday," 日没 *nichibotsu* "sunset," and 日食 *nisshoku* "solar eclipse," lit. "sun eating." The word for "lunar eclipse" is, logically enough, 月食 *gesshoku*.

Identical in pronunciation to 水星 *suisei* "Venus" is 彗星 *sui-sei* "comet." Meteoroids, i.e., small pieces of matter in outer space, are called 流星体 *ryūsei-tai*, lit. "floating star bodies." When these enter the earth's atmosphere as meteors, or "shooting stars," they are called 流星 *ryūsei* or 流れ星 *nagareboshi*;

should any part of them strike earth, they become 隕石 *inseki* "meteorites."

22. 僕の子供の時、雲に覆われている金星に生き物がいるのではないかと推測されていたが、最近その惑星の表面が「地獄*」ほど暑いことが明らかになった。

*Boku no kodomo no toki, kumo ni ōwarete iru **kinsei** ni ikimono ga iru no de wa nai ka to suisoku-sarete ita ga, saikin sono **wakusei** no hyōmen ga "jigoku" hodo atsui koto ga akiraka ni natta.*

When I was a child, there was speculation that there might be life on cloud-enshrouded Venus, but recently it has become clear that the surface of the planet is a virtual inferno.

> * *jigoku*: hell, hades; here referring to 炎熱地獄 *ennetsu-jigoku*, the hot part of Buddhist hell

23. 命名されている*3000個以上の小惑星は、主として火星と木星の軌道†の間にあります。

*Meimei sarete iru sanzen-ko ijō no **shō-wakusei** wa, shu to shite **kasei** to **mokusei** no kidō no aida ni arimasu.*

The asteroids, more than 3,000 of which have been identified and named, are found mainly between the orbits of Mars and Saturn.

> * *meimei suru*: to name
> † *kidō*: orbit

24. あるアメリカの古生物学者によると、恐竜*が約6000万年前に絶滅†したのは、巨大な隕石が地面に衝突◆した結果だそうです。

*Aru amerika no **koseibutsu-gaku**sha ni yoru to, kyōryū ga yaku rokusen-man-nen mae ni zetsumetsu shita no wa, kyodai na **inseki** ga jimen ni shōtotsu shita kekka da sō desu.*

According to certain American paleontologists, the dinosaurs became extinct as the result of a gigantic meteorite crashing into the earth's surface.

> * *kyōryū*: dinosaur (lit. terrible dragon)
> † *zetsumetsu*: extinction
> ◆ *shōtotsu*: collision

25. 人類最初の人工衛星は、1957年にソビエトが打ち上げた「スプートニク」でした。

*Jinrui-saisho no **jinkō-eisei** wa, sen-kyūhyaku-gojūshichi-nen ni sobieto ga uchiageta "supūtoniku" deshita.*

Mankind's first artificial satellite was the Sputnik, launched by the Soviet Union in 1957.

For scientists interested in learning Japanese for work in their specialized fields, recourse to technical dictionaries is, of course, essential. Still, the following representative list of terms found in a widely used middle school science textbook should be of general use. A few have already appeared in the illustrative sentences above.

物理学 (*butsuri-gaku*) physics

物体 (*buttai*) physical body, object

物質 (*busshitsu*) matter

速度 (*sokudo*) velocity

加速度 (*kasoku-do*) acceleration

減速度 (*gensoku-do*) deceleration

力 (*chikara*) power, force (read *-ryoku* in Sino-Japanese compounds)

重力 (*jūryoku*) gravity

圧力 (*atsuryoku*) pressure

浮力 (*furyoku*) buoyancy

慣性(力) (*kansei[-ryoku]*) inertia

慣性抵抗 (*kansei-teikō*) inertial resistance

遠心力 (*enshin-ryoku*) centrifugal force

求心力 (*kyūshin-ryoku*) centripetal force

火力 (*karyoku*) thermal power, caloric force

磁力 (*jiryoku*) magnetic force

原子力 (*genshi-ryoku*) nuclear power

地熱 (*jinetsu*) terrestrial heat, geotherm (also pronounced *chinetsu*)

風力 (*fūryoku*) wind force

波力 (*haryoku*) wave force

潮汐力 (*chōseki-ryoku*) tidal force

電力 (*denryoku*) electrical power

電圧 (*den'atsu*) voltage

電解 (*denkai*) electrolysis

電磁力 (*denji-ryoku*) electromagnetic force

電流 (*denryū*) electrical current

(電)磁石 (*[den-]jishaku*) (electro)magnet

エネルギー (*enerugī*) energy

位置エネルギー (*ichi-enerugī*) potential energy

運動エネルギー (*undō-enerugī*) kinetic energy

弾性のエネルギー (*dansei no enerugī*) elasticity

凝固点 (*gyōko-ten*) freezing point

融点 (*yūten*) melting point

温度 (*ondo*) temperature

湿度 (*shitsudo*) humidity

濃度 (*nōdo*) concentration

密度 (*mitsudo*) density

26. バスが急に止まると、立っている乗客は慣性の力によって前に倒れる。

*Basu ga kyū ni tomaru to, tatte iru jōkyaku wa **kansei** no chikara ni yotte mae ni taoreru.*

When a bus comes to a sudden stop, standing passengers are thrown forward by the force of inertia.

27. 塩水は真水より凝固点が低い。

*Shiomizu wa mamizu yori **gyōko-ten** ga hikui.*

Salt water has a lower freezing point than fresh water.

28. 安全性の問題を解決するまで、原子力発電所＊は増やさないほうがいいという意見が強まってきました。

*Anzen-sei no mondai o kaiketsu suru made, **genshi-ryoku**–hatsuden-sho wa fuyasanai hō ga ii to iu iken ga tsuyomatte kimashita.*

The view that nuclear power plants should not be increased until the question of their safety is resolved has been gaining ground.

＊ *hatsuden-sho*: power plant

化学 (*kagaku*) chemistry

固体 (*kotai*) solid

液体 (*ekitai*) liquid

気体 (*kitai*) gas

原子 (*genshi*) atom

原子核 (*genshi-kaku*) atomic nucleus

分子 (*bunshi*) molecule

元素 (*genso*) elements

　水素 (*suiso*) hydrogen (lit. water stuff)

　炭素 (*tanso*) carbon (lit. coal stuff)

　酸素 (*sanso*) oxygen (lit. sour stuff)

　窒素 (*chisso*) nitrogen (lit. suffocating stuff)

　臭素 (*shūso*) bromide (lit. stink stuff)

　ネオン (*neon*) neon

　ヘリウム (*heryūmu*) helium (*ri* + *u* → *ryū*)

　硼素 (*hōso*) boron

　燐 (*rin*) phosphorus

　沃素 (*yōso*) iodine

ナトリウム (*natoryūmu*) sodium (*ri + u → ryū*)

塩素 (*enso*) chlorine

亜鉛 (*aen*) zinc

アルミニウム (*aruminyūmu*) aluminum (*ni + u → nyū*)

カリウム (*karyūmu*) potassium (*ri + u → ryū*)

カルシウム (*karushūmu*) calcium (*shi + u → shū*)

金 (*kin*) gold

銀 (*gin*) silver

水銀 (*suigin*) mercury

錫 (*suzu*) tin (not to be confused with 鈴 *suzu* "bell")

鉄 (*tetsu*) iron

銅 (*dō*) copper

バリウム (*baryūmu*) barium (*ri + u → ryū*)

マグネシウム (*maguneshūmu*) magnesium (*shi + u → shū*)

マンガン (*mangan*) manganese

アルゴン (*arugon*) argon

硫黄 (*iō*) sulfur

珪素 (*keiso*) silicon

化合物 (*kagō-butsu*) chemical compound

硫化鉄 (*ryūka-tetsu*) iron sulfide

酸化鉄 (*sanka-tetsu*) iron oxide

青酸カリ (*seisan-kari*) potassium cyanide

硫酸 (*ryūsan*) sulfuric acid

塩酸 (*ensan*) hydrochloric acid

一酸化炭素 (*issan-ka–tanso*) carbon monoxide

二酸化炭素 (*nisan-ka–tanso*) carbon dioxide (also 炭酸ガス *tansan-gasu*)

酸と塩基 (*san to enki*) acids and bases

アルカリ (*arukari*) alkali

中和 (*chūwa*) neutralization [+ *suru*]

化学反応 (*kagaku-hannō*) chemical reaction

化学変化 (*kagaku-henka*) chemical change

化学分析 (*kagaku-bunseki*) chemical analysis

イオン (*ion*) ion

29. 酸化は、酸素が他の物質と化合*することです。例えば、赤錆びは主に酸化鉄と水酸化鉄とからなります。

Sanka wa, sanso ga hoka no busshitsu to kagō suru koto desu. Tatoeba, aka-sabi wa omo ni sanka-tetsu to sui–sanka-tetsu to kara narimasu.

Oxidation is the combining of oxygen and another substance. Rust, for example, consists mainly of ferric oxide and ferric hydroxide.

  * *kagō*: chemical combination

30. 青酸カリは猛毒なので、普通は手に入りません。

***Seisan-kari** wa mōdoku na no de, futsū wa te ni harimasen.*

As potassium cyanide is a deadly poison, it is not easily available..

31. 食塩は、塩化ナトリウム(NaCl)、つまりナトリウムと塩素との化合物です。

*Shokuen wa, enka-natoryūmu (NaCl), tsumari natoryūmu to enso to no **kagō-butsu** desu.*

Table salt is sodium chloride (NaCl), i.e., a compound of sodium and chlorine.

生物学 (*seibutsu-gaku*) biology

デオキシリボ核酸 (*deokishiribo-kakusan*) deoxyribonucleic acid (DNA)

ヌクレオチド (*nukureochido*) nucleotide

遺伝子 (*iden-shi*) gene (cf. 遺伝 *iden* "heredity")

染色体 (*senshoku-tai*) chromosome (lit. staining body)

細胞 (*saibō*) cell

細胞膜 (*saibō-maku*) cell membrane

細胞壁 (*saibō-heki*) cell wall

細胞分裂 (*saibō-bunretsu*) cell division

原形質 (*genkei-shitsu*) protoplasm

発生 (*hassei*) development, generation, breeding

生殖 (*seishoku*) reproduction

有性生殖 (*yūsei-seishoku*) sexual reproduction

無性生殖 (*musei-seishoku*) asexual reproduction

植物 (*shokubutsu*) plants

藻類 (*sōrui*) algae

苔類 (*kokerui*) lichen

羊歯類 (*shida-rui*) Pteridophyta, ferns

菌類 (*kinrui*) fungi

細菌 (*saikin*) bacilli, bacteria (more colloquial is ばい菌 *baikin*)

種子植物 (*shushi-shokubutsu*) seed-bearing plants

根 (*ne*) root

茎 (*kuki*) stem

葉 (*ha*) leaf

花 (*hana*) flower, blossom

葉緑素 (*yōroku-so*) chlorophyl

光合成 (*kō-gōsei*) photosynthesis

樹木 (*jumoku*) trees, arbores

柏 (*kashiwa*) oak

楓 (*kaede*) maple

椿 (*tsubaki*) camellia

桜 (*sakura*) cherry

松 (*matsu*) pine

杉 (*sugi*) cedar

樟/楠 (*kusu[noki]*) camphor

柳 (*yanagi*) willow

銀杏 (*ichō*) gingko

桐 (*kiri*) paulownia

草花 (*kusabana*; *sōka*) flowering plants

菊 (*kiku*) chrysanthemum

葵 (*aoi*) mallow, hollyhock

蓮 (*hasu*) lotus

蘭 (*ran*) orchid

藤 (*fuji*) wisteria

萩 (*hagi*) bush clover

菖蒲 (*shōbu*) iris

葦 (*ashi*; *yoshi*) reed, bulrush

藍 (*ai*) indigo plant

蓼 (*tade*) polygonum, smartweed

動物 (*dōbutsu*) animals

無脊椎動物 (*mu-sekitsui–dōbutsu*) invertebrates

原生動物 (*gensei-dōbutsu*) Protozoa

腔腸動物 (*kōchō-dōbutsu*) Coelenterata (lit. hollow intestine)

棘皮動物 (*kyokuhi-dōbutsu*) Echinodermata (lit. thorn skin)

海綿動物 (*kaimen-dōbutsu*) Porifera (lit. sea cotton)

扁形動物 (*henkei-dōbutsu*) Plathelminthes (lit. flat shape)

環形動物 (*kankei-dōbutsu*) Annelida

軟体動物 (*nantai-dōbutsu*) Mollusca (lit. soft body)

節足動物 (*sessoku-dōbutsu*) Arthropoda (lit. joint leg)

昆虫類 (*konchū-rui*) Insecta

蜘蛛類 (*kumo-rui*) Arachnida

甲殻類 (*kōkaku-rui*) Crustacea

脊椎動物 (*sekitsui-dōbutsu*) vertebrates

魚類 (*gyorui*) Pisces (fish)

両棲類 (*ryōsei-rui*) Amphibia

爬虫類 (*hachū-rui*) Reptilia (lit. scratching vermin)

鳥類 (*chōrui*) Aves (birds)

哺乳類 (*honyū-rui*) Mammalia

32. 光合成は、植物が太陽エネルギーを用いて澱粉を作る過程です。

*Kō-gōsei wa, **shokubutsu** ga taiyō-enerugī o mochiite denpun o tsukuru katei desu.*

Photosynthesis is the process whereby plants produce starch, using solar energy.

33. 学生に最もよく知られている微生物は、おそらくアメーバです。

*Gakusei ni mottomo yoku shirarete iru **bi-seibutsu** wa, osoraku amēba desu.*

The microorganism most familiar to students is probably the amoeba.

34. 私は、クモ学者と結婚するまでクモが昆虫類に属していないことを知りませんでした。

*Watashi wa, **kumo**gaku-sha to kekkon suru made **kumo** ga **konchū-rui** ni zoku-shite inai koto o shirimasen deshita.*

Until I married an arachnologist, I was unaware that spiders do not belong to the insect family.

35. 鮫と違って、イルカと鯨は魚類ではなく哺乳動物です。

*Same to chigatte, iruka to kujira wa **gyorui** de wa naku **honyū-dōbutsu** desu.*

Unlike the shark, the dolphin and the whale are not fish but mammals.

Chapter
VI

Law and Justice

Corruptissima republica plurimae leges, wrote the Roman historian Tacitus: 国家が堕落すればするほどその法律が多くなる *Kokka ga daraku sureba suru hodo sono hōritsu ga ōku naru* "The more corrupt the state, the more numerous its laws." To Lao Tze, Tacitus' *senpai* by some seven centuries, is attributed a saying which, if turned around, sounds somewhat similar: 法令滋影盗賊多有. Translated into Japanese, this becomes 法令益々彰かにして、盗賊多し *Hōrei masumasu akiraka ni shite, tōzoku ōshi* "To specify the laws is to multiply the bandits."

If all this is true, we moderns certainly live in evil times! As Cicero put it, *o tempora, o mores!* or この時代とその慣習よ! *Kono jidai to sono kanshū yo!* "Oh these times and their manners!"

While this chapter will make of no one a lawyer, it should provide the basics for making one's way (in Japanese) through our legally complex world. Once again, we begin with a few lexical building blocks. As in other chapters, these are predominantly of Sino-Japanese origin, for much as the English have borrowed their legal vocabulary from Romance sources (French and Latin), so the Japanese have taken theirs from Chinese.

Laws, Ordinances, Orders, and Regulations
法 HŌ • 律 RITSU • 令 REI • 則 SOKU

The semantic range of 法 *hō*, whose meaning in Ancient Chinese (**piap*) was originally "constraint, confinement," extends beyond the arm of the law to include "method, Buddhist [doctrine]." Examples more relevant to our immediate concerns here are the following:

法(律) (*hō[ritsu]*) law

法令 (*hōrei*) legislation, laws

法案 (*hōan*) legislative proposal

法(理)学 (*hō[ri-]gaku*) jurisprudence, cf. 法哲学 *hōtetsu-gaku*

法曹(界) (*hōsō[-kai]*) (the world of) the legal profession

法務省 (*hōmu-shō*) the Ministry of Justice

法治 (*hōchi*) constitutional government

法廷 (*hōtei*) court of law

合法 (*gōhō*) legality

違法 (*ihō*) illegality

立法 (*rippō*) lawmaking, legislation

司法 (*shihō*) administration of justice

憲法 (*kenpō*) constitution

1. 法の前では万人が平等です。

Hō no mae de wa bannin ga byōdō desu.

All are equal before the law.

2. 野党が法案を提出しても、可決*される可能性はほとんどありません。

*Yatō ga **hōan** o teishutsu shite mo, kaketsu sareru kanō-sei wa hotondo arimasen.*

Even if the opposition parties submit legislative proposals, the chances of their passage are virtually nil.

* *kaketsu*: approval, adoption

3. 秋本さんは、法曹界で有名な人物です。

*Akimoto-san wa, **hōsō-kai** de yūmei na jinbutsu desu.*

Mr. Akimoto is a well-known person in Japanese legal circles.

4. 祖父は、戦後の憲法を「米国に押し付けられた*」と非難していますが、母は、憲法擁護運動の熱心な支持者です。

*Sofu wa, sengo no **kenpō** o "beikoku ni oshitsukerareta" to hinan shite imasu ga, haha wa, kenpō–yōgo-undō no nesshin na shiji-sha desu.*

Grandfather denounces Japan's postwar Constitution as "imposed by the Americans," but my mother is a zealous supporter of the movement to protect and preserve it.

* *oshitsukeru*: to force upon

5. この地方の警察は、違法駐車を黙認しているような気がします。

*Kono chihō no keisatsu wa, **ihō**-chūsha o mokunin shite iru yō na ki ga shimasu.*

My impression is that the regional police turn a blind eye to illegally parked cars.

The multiple uses of 法 *hō* make for some unpredictability in the meaning of compounds. One of these is as the Chinese translation of Sanskrit *dharma* "cosmic law, principle," referring to Buddhism or Buddhist teachings. Thus, for example, 法事 *hōji* does not refer to legal affairs but rather to a Buddhist memorial service. Another problem is the difference between "law" and "method," which, though seemingly minor, is crucial in such terms as 避妊法 *hinin-hō*, which pertains to birth control methods, not to laws regarding contraception. In the case of 商法 *shōhō*, context alone will determine whether the meaning is "commercial law" or "way of doing business."

In the following, 法 *-hō* is used to designate categories of the law, along with statutes and legislative acts.

刑(事)法 (*kei[ji-]hō*) criminal law

民(事)法 (*min[ji-hō]pō*) civil law

軍法 (*gunpō*) military law

会社法 (*kaisha-hō*) corporation/company law

法例法 (*hōrei-hō*) case law

不法行為法 (*fuhō-kōi-hō*) tort law

国法 (*kokuhō*) national law(s)

国際法 (*kokusai-hō*) international law

刑事訴訟法 (*keiji–sosho-hō*) Criminal Procedure Act

破壊活動防止法 (*hakai-katsudō–bōshi-hō*) the Anti-Subversive Activities Act

売春防止法 (*baishun–bōshi-hō*) the Anti-Prostitution Act

汚職防止法 (*oshoku–bōshi-hō*) the Corrupt Practices Prevention Act

独占禁止法 (*dokusen–kinshi-hō*) the Anti-Monopoly Act

外国為替及び外国貿易管理法 (*gaikoku-kawase–oyobi–gaikoku-boeki–kanri-hō*) the Foreign Exchange and Foreign Trade Control Act

建物保護法 (*tatemono–hogo-hō*) the Building Preservation Act

借地法 (*shakuchi-hō*) the Land Lease Act

地方公務員法 (*chihō–kōmuin-hō*) Local Officials Act

麻薬取締法 (*mayaku–torishimari-hō*) the Narcotics Control Act

犯罪者予防更生法 (*hanzaisha-yobō-kōsei-hō*) the Corrective and Reformative Treatment of Criminals Act

出入国管理及び難民認定法 *shutsunyū-koku-kanri–oyobi–nanmin-nintei-hō*) Immigration Control and Refugee Recognition Law

男女雇用機会均等法 (*danjo-koyō-kikai-kintō-hō*) the Equal Employment Opportunity Law (men and women)

6. アメリカのエリート法学部を出た弟は、不法行為法の専門家です。

Amerika no erīto–hōgaku-bu o deta otōto wa, **fuhō-kōi-hō** *no senmon-ka desu.*

My younger brother, a product of a top American law school, is a specialist in tort law.

7. 日本の売春防止法が成立したのは、1956年でした。

Nihon no **baishun–bōshi-hō** *ga seiritsu shita no wa, sen-kyūhyaku-gojūroku-nen deshita.*

Japan's Anti-Prostitution Law was passed in 1956.

8. 国会が男女雇用機会均等法に罰則＊を設けなかった†ので、空文だという意見があります。

Kokkai ga **danjo-koyō-kikai-kintō-hō** *ni bassoku o mōkenakatta no de, kūbun da to iu iken ga arimasu.*

As the Diet did not put any teeth into the Equal Employment Opportunity Law, some are of the opinion that it is a mere scrap of paper.

＊ *bassoku*: penal regulations
† *mōkeru*: establish, lay down

9. アメリカ合衆国の憲法が特徴とする立法・行政・司法の三権分立＊の目的は、国民の自由を保障することです。

Amerika–gasshū-koku no kenpō ga tokuchō to suru **rippō**, *gyōsei,* **shihō** *no sanken-bunritsu no mokuteki wa, kokumin no jiyū o hoshō suru koto desu.*

The purpose of the separation of powers—legislative, executive, and judicial—a characteristic of the Constitution of the United States, is to ensure the liberty of the people.

＊ *sanken-bunritsu*: separation of powers

律 *ritsu* "law, discipline," Ancient Chinese **liuet*, became prominent in Japanese no later than the beginning of the eighth century, thereby predating by several hundred years the introduction into English of Old Norse *lagu* [> law]. An example of historical significance is 律令 *ritsuryō/ritsurei*, the term for the laws and ordinances of the Nara and Heian periods.

規律 (*kiritsu*) order, discipline
軍律 (*gunritsu*) martial law, martial discipline

成文律 (*seibun-ritsu*) statute, established law

不文律 (*fubun-ritsu*) unwritten law

黄金律 (*ōgon-ritsu*) the Golden Rule

戒律 (*kairitsu*) religious precepts (Buddhist)

律法 (*rippō*) = *kairitsu* (Buddhist); Torah (Judaism), Shariah (Islam)

道徳律 (*dōtoku-ritsu*) moral code

反律法主義 (*hanrippō-shugi*) antinomianism (< Greek *anti* + *nomos* "law")

Like Greek *nomos*, *ritsu* extends beyond the social or political sense of law to include musical and poetical form, e.g., 旋律 *senritsu* "melody" (cf. Ch. 4), 音律 *onritsu* "tune," and 韻律 *inritsu* "rhythm, meter." This helps to explain why a 調律師 *chōritsu-shi* is not an "investigative legalist" but rather a "piano tuner."

10. 「十戒*」は、モーゼの律法の基本です。

*"Jikkai" wa mōze no **rippō** no kihon desu.*

The Ten Commandments are the foundation of Mosaic Law.

　　* *jikkai*: the Ten Commandments, also the Ten Buddhist Precepts

11. 僕の哲学の教授は、ニーチェを引用して道徳律をいつもあざけって*いたが、奥さんが若い講師に誘惑され†家出した時、彼女をふしだらな女だと非難した。

*Boku no tetsugaku no kyōju wa, nīche o in'yō shite **dōtoku-ritsu** o itsumo azakette ita ga, okusan ga wakai kōshi ni yūwaku sare iede shita toki, kanojo o fushidara na onna da to hinan shita.*

My philosophy professor was wont to quote Nietzsche and ridicule moral codes, but when his wife was seduced by a young lecturer and ran away from home, he denounced her as a slut.

　　* *azakeru*: sneer (jeer) at, ridicule
　　† *yūwaku suru*: tempt, seduce

12. 「何事も人にせられん*と思うことは人にもそのごとくせよ」という言葉は、「黄金律」と呼ばれます。

*"Nani-goto mo hito ni seraren to omou koto wa hito ni mo sono gotoku seyo" to iu kotoba wa, "**ōgon-ritsu**" to yobaremasu.*

The words "All things whatsoever ye would that men should do to you, do ye even so to them" are known as the "Golden Rule."

　　* *seraren = saretai*

令 *rei* "order, command," which as Ancient Chinese *lieng meant "purity," is used as a prefix in such polite expressions as 令嬢 *reijō* "your daughter, young lady" and 令息 *reisoku* "your son," but in 令状 *reijō*, the meaning is not "fine condition" or "your letter" but rather "warrant," as in 逮捕令状 *taiho-reijō* "arrest warrant." Above we also saw the historical example of 律令, "laws and ordinances," read as either *ritsuryō* or *ritsurei*. Other compounds include:

命令 (*meirei*) command

勅令 (*chokurei*) Imperial edict

政令 (*seirei*) government ordinance, cabinet order

訓令 (*kunrei*) directive

司令長官 (*shirei-chōkan*) Commander-in-Chief

徴兵令 (*chōhei-rei*) conscription/draft

戒厳令 (*kaigen-rei*) martial law

13. マッカーサー在朝鮮国連軍最高司令官は、1951年にトルーマン大統領の命令に背いたため、解任された。

*Makkāsā zai-chōsen-kokuren-gun saikō-shirei-kan wa, sen-kyū-hyaku-gojūichi-nen ni torūman-daitōryō no **meirei** ni somuita tame, kainin sareta.*

(Douglas) MacArthur, Supreme Commander of the United Nations Forces in Korea, was dismissed in 1951 for defying President Truman's orders.

14. マルコス・フィリピン大統領が1972年に戒厳令を敷いた時、兄とそのフィリピン人の奥さんはマニラに住んでいました。

*Marukosu firipin daitōryō ga sen-kyūhyaku-nanajūni-nen ni **kaigen-rei** o shiita toki, ani to sono firipin-jin no okusan wa manira ni sunde imashita.*

When Philippine President Marcos declared martial law in 1972, my elder brother and his Filipina wife were living in Manila.

則 *soku* "rule, law, regulation," derived from Ancient Chinese *tsək "conformity, pertinence," occurs, with one prominent exception, in noninitial position.

則天去私 (*sokuten-kyoshi*) selfless devotion (lit. submission to heaven, abandoning self)

原則 (*gensoku*) principle

規則 (*kisoku*) rule

罰則 (*bassoku*) penal regulations

獄則 (*gokusoku*) prison regulations

校則 (*kōsoku*) school regulations

法則 (*hōsoku*) (scientific) law

15. この団地では、犬や猫を飼うことは原則として禁止されていますが、実際には飼っている人が最近多くなっています。

*Kono danchi de wa, inu ya neko o kau koto wa **gensoku** toshite kinshi sarete imasu ga, jissai ni wa katte iru hito ga saikin ōku natte imasu.*

Keeping dogs or cats in this apartment complex is, in principle, prohibited, but in fact the number of such pet owners has recently increased.

16. 女性がクラブの会員になってはいけないという規則は考え直すべきだと会長に意見を言いました。

*Josei ga kurabu no kai'in ni natte wa ikenai to iu **kisoku** wa kangae-naosu beki da to kaichō ni iken o iimashita.*

I told the club president that in my opinion the rule barring women as members should be reconsidered.

17. 自然の法則は、人間の法律よりずっと精妙にできていると思います。

*Shizen no **hōsoku** wa, ningen no hōritsu yori zutto seimyō ni dekite iru to omoimasu.*

The laws of nature are vastly more subtle and intricate than the laws of men.

Two native Japanese words that should be included here are *nori* and *okite*. The first derives from 宣る *noru* "utter, declare (of a god or emperor)," cf. 則る *nottoru* "follow, live up to, conform to (a rule)." The second is a nominalized form of *okitsu* "set forth and build up." (Note the etymological resemblance between law [lay] and *okite* [*oku* "lay"].) *Nori*, particularly as it appears in personal names, is written with a variety of characters, including 則 *soku*, 憲 *ken*, 法 *hō*, and even 徳 *toku* ("virtue"). Even more than Sino-Japanese *hō*, it is closely associated with religious, especially Buddhist, exhortations to good behavior.

18. 「法の道* 入るべき門は　変れども　つひには同じ　悟りとぞ聞く」（新後拾遺和歌集）

*"**Nori** no michi / iru-beki kado wa / kaware-domo / tsui ni wa onaji / satori to zo kiku." (Shingoshūi-wakashū New Later Collection of Gleanings*, fourteenth century)

Though the gate that leadeth into the Way to the Law may vary, the message of enlightenment remains the same.

* *nori no michi*: the Way to the Law = Buddhist teachings

Like *nori*, *okite* 掟 has a somewhat archaic ring to it. The glosses offered by *Kenkyusha* suggest a broad range of meaning: "rule, law, regulation, statute, institution, decree, commandment."

19. 一宿一飯の恩義*に報いる†のがやくざの掟だ。

Isshuku-ippan no ongi ni mukuiru no ga yakuza no okite da.

A precept of Japanese gangsterdom is that (so small an act of kindness as) a single night's lodging and a meal should be rewarded.

* *ongi*: a favor, a debt of gratitude
† *mukuiru*: to requite, repay

20. ジャングルの掟は、「弱肉強食」という原則に基づいている。

*Janguru no **okite** wa, "jakuniku-kyōshoku" to iu **gensoku** ni motozuite iru.*

The law of the jungle is based on the principle that the strong devour the weak.

Law and Order
法と秩序   HŌ TO CHITSUJO

Having looked at various rather abstract words for "law," we now turn to the legal "order" (秩序 *chitsujo*) itself. We begin in the courtroom.

法廷 (*hōtei*) court of law (also 裁判所 *saiban-sho*)

裁判 (*saiban*) trial

訴訟 (*soshō*) lawsuit

裁判官 (*saiban-kan*) judge (also 判事 *hanji*)

検事 (*kenji*) prosecutor

検察 (*kensatsu*) prosecution

起訴 (*kiso*) indictment (+ *suru*)

弁護人 (*bengo-nin*) defense attorney

弁護士 (*bengo-shi*) lawyer

被告人 (*hikoku-nin*) the accused, defendant

証拠 (*shōko*) evidence

証人 (*shōnin*) witness

証言 (*shōgen*) testimony (+ *suru*)

求刑 (*kyūkei*) prosecution's penalty recommendation

判決 (*hanketsu*) verdict

   有罪判決 (*yūzai-hanketsu*) verdict of guilty

   無罪判決 (*muzai-hanketsu*) verdict of innocent

宣告 (*senkoku*) sentence

控訴 (*kōso*) appeal

21. 息子の同級生は過激派*のテロ活動に連座した†かど◆で、被告
人として裁判にかけられた✿ことがありますが、結局無罪判決
を受けました。

*Musuko no dōkyū-sei wa kageki-ha no tero-katsudō ni renza shita
kado de, **hikoku-nin** to shite **saiban** ni kakerareta koto ga arimasu ga, kekkyoku **muzai-hanketsu** o ukemashita.*

A university classmate of my son was once implicated in terrorists
activities and brought to trial. In the end, he was found innocent.

> * *kageki-ha*: (left-wing) extremists
> † *renza suru*: lit. "to sit together"; to be involved, implicated (cf. 連座制 *renza-sei*
> "guilt-by-association system"
> ◆ *kado*: grounds, suspicion, charge
> ✿ *saiban ni kakeru*: take to court, put on trial

22. 日本人から見れば、アメリカ人は非常に訴訟好きな国民です。

*Nihon-jin kara mireba, amerika-jin wa hijō ni **soshō**-zuki na kokumin desu.*

From the Japanese point of view, Americans are a terribly litigious
people.

23. 容疑者*の指紋†が包丁◆に残っていたことが、検察側にとって
決定的な証拠になったらしい。

*Yōgi-sha no shimon ga hōchō ni nokotte ita koto ga, **kensatsu-
gawa** ni totte kettei-teki na **shōko** ni natta rashii.*

The prosecution seems to regard the fact that the suspect's finger-
prints were left on the knife as decisive evidence.

> * *yōgi-sha*: suspect
> † *shimon*: fingerprints
> ◆ *hōchō*: kitchen knife

24. 警察は、真弓が愛人に殺されたのではないかと疑っているかも
しれないが、直接の証拠がない限りその男を逮捕することはで
きない。

*Keisatsu wa, mayumi ga aijin ni korosareta no de wa nai ka to uta-
gatte iru kamo shirenai ga, chokusetsu no **shōko** ga nai kagiri
sono otoko o taiho suru koto wa dekinai.*

The police may suspect that Mayumi was murdered by her lover,
but as long as they have no hard evidence, they can't arrest
him.

25. 被告人が被害者*を橋から突き落としたと証言できる目撃者†は
十数人います。

***Hikoku-nin** ga higai-sha o hashi kara tsukiotoshita to **shōgen** de-
kiru mokugeki-sha wa jū-sū-nin imasu.*

There are more than ten eyewitnesses who can testify that the
accused pushed the victim off the bridge.

> * *higai-sha*: victim
> † *mokugeki-sha*: eyewitness

26. 有罪と判決されるまで被告人を無罪だと推定するのは、アング
    ロサクソン法の基礎です。

*Yūzai to hanketsu sareru made **hikoku-nin** o **muzai** da to suitei
suru no wa, angurosakuson-hō no kiso desu.*

The presumption that a defendant is innocent until proven guilty
lies at the foundation of Anglo-Saxon Law.

27. 銀行強盗*で起訴された山田勉被告に対して、検事は15年の懲
    役†を求刑しました。

*Ginkō-gōtō de kiso sareta yamada tsutomu hikoku ni taishite, kenji
wa jūgo-nen no chōeki o **kyūkei** shimashita.*

The prosecution proposed fifteen years at forced labor for Tsutomu
Yamada, under indictment for bank robbery.

  * *gōtō*: mugging, armed robbery
  † *chōeki*: imprisonment at forced labor

As in the preceding example, the media typically refer to
the accused as … 被告 … *hikoku*. For more on 懲役 *chōeki*
"forced labor," see "Crime and Punishment" below.

28. 信仰上の理由により剣道の授業に参加するのを断ったため退学
    処分*を受けた大学生は、一審で敗訴しましたが、当然控訴す
    るでしょう。

*Shinkō-jō no riyū ni yori kendō no jugyō ni sanka suru no o koto-
watta tame taigaku-shobun o uketa daigaku-sei wa, isshin de
haiso shimashita ga, tōzen **kōso** suru deshō.*

The students who were expelled from the university for refusing to
participate in Japanese fencing classes because of their religious faith have lost their lawsuit, but they are sure to appeal.

  * *shobun*: disposal, punishment

The hierarchical structure of the Japanese court system,
from the highest to the lowest, is as follows:

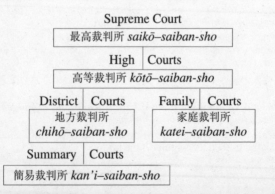

Supreme Court
最高裁判所 *saikō–saiban-sho*

High | Courts
高等裁判所 *kōtō–saiban-sho*

District | Courts — Family | Courts
地方裁判所 *chihō–saiban-sho* — 家庭裁判所 *katei–saiban-sho*

Summary | Courts
簡易裁判所 *kan'i–saiban-sho*

29. アメリカの最高裁判事は大統領に指名され、上院で承認されますが、日本では内閣で任命されます。

*Amerika no **saikō-sai**–hanji wa daitōryō ni shimei sare, jōin de shōnin saremasu ga, nihon de wa naikaku de ninmei saremasu.*

America's Supreme Court justices are nominated by the president and confirmed by the Senate, but in Japan they are appointed by the Cabinet.

30. 離婚する時、家庭裁判所に養育権訴訟＊を起こす男の人が最近増えてきたそうです。

*Rikon suru toki, **katei–saiban-sho** ni yōiku-ken–soshō o okosu otoko no hito ga saikin fuete kita sō desu.*

There has apparently been a recent increase in the number of men filing child custody suits with the family courts at the time of divorce.

＊ *yōiku-ken–soshō*: child custody suit

Crime and Punishment
罪(犯罪)と(刑)罰　TSUMI (HANZAI) TO (KEI)BATSU

As suggested by「罪と罰」, the Japanese translation of the title of Dostoevski's famous novel, the semantic range of 罪 *tsumi* includes "crime" as well as "sin." Still, the usual word for the former is Sino-Japanese 犯罪 *hanzai*, lit. "doing wrong." The characters themselves have an ominous air about them: the first contains the "beast" or "dog" radical, the second the "net" radical, grim reminders of the nature and destiny of 犯罪者 *hanzai-sha* "criminals" in traditional East Asian society.

軽罪 (*keizai*) minor offense (not to be confused with 経済 *keizai* "economics")

重罪 (*jūzai*) grave offense

窃盗罪 (*settō-zai*) larceny, cf. native Japanese 盗み *nusumi* "theft"

万引き (*manbiki*) shoplifting

すり (*suri*) pickpocket(ing)

ひったくり (*hittakuri*) purse-snatching/purse-snatcher

詐欺 (*sagi*) fraud, cf. 詐欺師 *sagi-shi* "swindler"

故買 (*kobai*) dealing in stolen goods

金庫破り (*kinko-yaburi*) safecracking

強盗 (*gōtō*) armed robbery, mugging

強盗犯人 (*gōtō-hannin*) armed robber, mugger

31. おえらいさん*の息子でも構いません。ひき逃げ運転は重罪で
すよ。

*Oerai-san no musuko de mo kamaimasen. Hikinige-unten wa **jūzai**
desu yo.*

I don't care if he's the son of a big shot. Hit-and-run driving is a
grave offense.

　＊ *oerai-san*: bigwig; from the adjective *erai* "admirable, great, highly placed"

32. アマト先生のお母さんは、昨日の夜オペラから帰って来る途中
でひったくりにハンドバッグを盗られてしまいました。

*Amato-sensei no okāsan wa, kinō no yoru opera kara kaette kuru
tochū de **hittakuri** ni handobaggu o torarete shimaimashita.*

Professor Amato's mother had her handbag taken by a purse-
snatcher on her way home from the opera last night.

　強要罪 (*kyōyō-zai*) extortion

　暴力犯罪 (*bōryoku-hanzai*) crime of violence

　性犯罪 (*sei-hanzai*) sex crime

　　猥褻罪 (*waisetsu-zai*) lascivious behavior, indecent expo-
　　　sure

　　強制猥褻罪 (*kyōsei–waisetsu-zai*) indecent assault

　　幼児猥褻罪 (*yōji–waisetsu-zai*) child molestation

　　強姦 (*gōkan*) rape

Like English "assault," 暴行 *bōkō* (lit. violent action) is still
used as a slightly less stark term for rape. Recently, Anglo-
Japanese レイプ *reipu* has also become "fashionable," particularly in the media.

Meanwhile, the lamentable catalog of human crime continues:

　殺人罪 (*satsujin-zai*) homicide

　　謀殺 (*bōsatsu*) premeditated murder

　　衝動殺人 (*shōdō-satsujin*) murder on impulse

　　殺人未遂 (*satsujin-misui*) attempted murder

　　過失致死 (*kashitsu-chishi*) involuntary manslaughter

　業務上過失致死罪 (*gyōmu-jō kashitsu-chishizai*) dereliction
　　of duty resulting in death

-殺し *-goroshi* "killing" corresponds to English *-cide*: 父殺し
chichi-goroshi "patricide," 兄弟殺し *kyōdai-goroshi* "fratricide,"
and 嬰児殺し *eiji-goroshi* "infanticide." Note, however, that the
suffix is used only in reference to the termination of human life.

If you are looking for an insecticide or a germicide, you must ask for 殺虫剤 *satchū-zai* or 殺菌剤 *sakkin-zai*.

33. 承諾*があったとしても、40歳の大人が女子高校生と性行為をすれば、やはり一種†の強姦でしかないと思うわ。

*Shōdaku ga atta to shite mo, yonjussai no otona ga joshi–kōkō-sei to sei-kōi o sureba, yahari isshu no **gōkan** de shika nai to omou wa.*

Even if it is consensual, I think that when a forty-year-old adult has sexual relations with a high school girl, it is nothing other than a form of rape.

* *shōdaku*: agreement, consent
† *isshu*: a kind, sort, variety

34. 愛人の殺人未遂で逮捕された吉田哲二は、自殺を図ったそうです。

*Aijin no **satsujin-misui** de taiho sareta yoshida tetsuji wa, jisatsu o hakatta sō desu.*

Tetsuji Yoshida, arrested for the attempted murder of his lover, has allegedly attempted suicide.

35. 飲酒運転で逮捕された上田裕治元電車運転士は、業務上過失致死罪で起訴されました。

*Inshu-unten de taiho sareta ueda yūji moto–densha-untenshi wa, **gyōmu-jō kashitsu-chishizai** de kiso saremashita.*

Former train operator Yuji Ueda, arrested for operating a train in an intoxicated condition, has been indicted for dereliction of duty resulting in death.

偽造 (*gizō*) forgery, counterfeiting; cf. 偽造者 *gizō-sha* "forger, counterfeiter"

誘拐 (*yūkai*) kidnapping, cf. 誘拐犯 *yūkai-han* "kidnapper"

放火 (*hōka*) arson, cf. 放火魔 *hōka-ma* "arsonist, pyromaniac"

ハイジャック (*haijakku*) hijacking, cf. 乗っ取り *nottori* same meaning

テロリズム (*terorizumu*) terrorism

麻薬(の)取引き (*mayaku [no] torihiki*) drug trafficking

密輸入 (*mitsu-yunyū*) smuggling

36. 金田社長を誘拐した犯人が要求している身代金*は 2 億円だそうです。

*Kaneda-shacho o **yukai** shita hannin ga yōkyū shite iru minoshiro-kin wa ni-oku-en da sō desu.*

The kidnappers of Company President Kaneda are said to be demanding ¥200 million in ransom.

* *minoshiro-kin*: ransom

37. これは素人でもすぐ気づくような偽造紙幣です。

*Kore wa shirōto de mo sugu kizuku yō na **gizō**-shihei desu.*

This, as even a layman will immediately realize, is a counterfeit note.

38. 3年前にマレーシアで麻薬を密輸入しようとして捕まり、死刑
   を宣告された*オーストラリア人は、来週処刑される†予定です。

*Sannen mae ni marēshia de mayaku o **mitsu-yunyū** shiyō to shite tsukamari, shikei o senkoku sareta ōsutoraria-jin wa, raishū shokei sareru yotei desu.*

The Australian who was caught trying to smuggle narcotics into Malaysia and sentenced to death is scheduled to be executed next week.

   * *shikei o senkoku sareru*: to be sentenced to death
   † *shokei sareru*: to be executed

If you look up 知能犯 *chinō-han* in Kenkyusha's *New Japanese-English Dictionary*, you may be perplexed or at least amused to find it glossed as "intellectual [mental] offense." In fact, the term refers neither to 思想犯 *shisō-han* "thought offense" under Japanese militarism nor to violations of political correctness on today's American university campuses but rather to what the American criminologist Edwin H. Sutherland back in 1949 called "white collar crime," of which ホワイトカラー族の犯罪 *howaito-karā-zoku no hanzai* is a more literal but less common translation. Examples include 偽造 *gizō* and 詐欺 *sagi* (above) as well as the following:

横領 (*ōryō*) embezzlement
インサイダー取引き (*insaidā-torihiki*) insider trading
背任 (*hainin*) breach of trust
脱税 (*datsuzei*) tax evasion
贈収賄 (*zōshū-wai*) giving and accepting bribes
   贈賄 (*zōwai*) offering bribes
   収賄 (*shūwai*) accepting bribes
不正資金浄化 (*fusei-shikin-jōka*) money laundering

The general term for corruption in the public sector is 汚職 *oshoku*, lit. "sullying (one's) office," cf. 汚職防止法 *oshoku-bōshi-hō* "Corrupt Practices Prevention Act" (above).

39. 日本の公務員は評判が良く、滅多に賄賂を受けたりなどする汚
   職事件に巻き込まれないが, 政治家についてはそうは言えない。

*Nihon no kōmuin wa hyōban ga yoku, metta ni wairo o uketari nado suru **oshoku**-jiken ni makikomarenai ga, seiji-ka ni tsuite wa sō wa ienai.*

*nado suru **oshoku**-jiken ni makikomarenai ga, seiji-ka ni tsuite wa sō wa ienai.*

Japanese civil servants have a good reputation and are seldom involved in bribe taking and other forms of corruption. The same, however, cannot be said of politicians.

"Are there no prisons?" asks Dickens' Scrooge of his portly gentlemen visitors. In Japanese, with due consideration for the setting, this is rendered as 「監獄はないんですかねえ」 *Kangoku wa nai n' desu ka nē*. Yet though the term for "prison law" is still known as 監獄法 *kangoku-hō*, of the actual incarceration facilities themselves, at least in official usage, are called 刑務所 *keimu-sho* "penitentiary" and 拘置所 *kōchi-sho* "detention center." The lockup for persons being held in police custody for interrogation is called a 留置場 *ryūchi-jō*.

Japanese law provides for three primary classes of punishment: death (死刑 *shikei*), imprisonment (投獄 *tōgoku*), and fines (罰金 *bakkin*). Of the second form, two subcategories are distinguished: confinement (禁固 *kinko*) without forced labor and imprisonment at forced labor (懲役 *chōeki*).

40. 一昨年不法入国*と強盗の疑いで捕まった男は、現在拘置所にいますが、来月自国へ強制送還†される予定です。

*Ototoshi fuhō-nyūkoku to gōtō no utagai de tsukamatta otoko wa, genzai **kōchi-sho** ni imasu ga, raigetsu jikoku e kyōsei-sōkan sareru yotei desu.*

The man who was caught illegally entering Japan and committing armed robbery is still in the detention center, but next month he is to be deported to his country of origin.
* *fuhō-nyūkoku*: illegal immigration
† *kyōsei-sōkan*: deportation

41. 日本では、死刑囚を処刑するためには法務大臣が死刑執行令状*に印を押す必要があります。

*Nihon de wa, shikei-shū o shokei suru tame ni wa hōmu-daijin ga **shikei–shikkō-reijō** ni in o osu hitsuyō ga arimasu.*

In Japan, it is necessary for the justice minister to affix his seal to the death warrant before a condemned convict can be executed.
* *shikei–shikkō-reijō*: death warrant

42. 飲酒運転をして過失致死罪に問われた*内藤奈々江は、2年の禁固刑に処せられました†。

*Inshu-unten o shite kashitsu–chishi-zai ni towareta naitō nanae wa, ninen no **kinko**-kei ni shoseraremashita.*

Charged with involuntary manslaughter while driving drunk, Nanae Naitō was sentenced to two years in prison.

* *tsumi ni towareru*: to be accused of (charged with) a crime
† *shosuru*: condemn, sentence

43. 新自由党元副幹事長佐藤敏樹は、選挙違反で禁固3ヵ月、執行猶
予*1年の判決を受けました。

*Shin–jiyū–tō moto–fuku–kanjichō satō toshiki wa, senkyo-ihan de **kinko**
san-ka-getsu, shikkō-yūyo ichi-nen no hanketsu o ukemashita.*

Toshiki Satō, former deputy secretary general of the New Freedom
Party, has been sentenced to three months imprisonment for
election violations, with a one-year suspension.

* *shikkō-yūyo*: sentence suspension

44. 車で時速160キロを出した兄は、警察に捕まって15万円の罰金
を取られました。

*Kuruma de jisoku hyaku-rokujukkiro o dashita ani wa, keisatsu ni
tsukamatte jūgo-man-en no **bakkin** o torareta.*

My elder brother was caught driving at 160 kilometers per hour by
the police and fined ¥150,000.

The policeman who clocks you or your elder brother for
speeding is most likely to be an ordinary 交通巡査 *kōtsū-junsa*
"traffic cop." In the fictional world of Japan's many police dra-
mas, the dashing investigator may be called 刑事さん *keiji-san*,
lit. "Mr. Detective," at least by some of the shadier characters,
but in reality, the term is closer in spirit to the American rather
than the Japanese system. A *junsa*'s superiors, in ascending
order, are as follows:

巡査長 (*junsa-chō*) senior policeman
巡査部長 (*junsa-buchō*) police sergeant
警部補 (*keibu-ho*) assistant police inspector
警部 (*keibu*) police inspector
警視 (*keishi*) superintendent
警視正 (*keishi-sei*) senior superintendent
警視長 (*keishi-chō*) chief superintendent
警視監 (*keishi-kan*) superintendent supervisor
警視総監 (*keishi-sōkan*) superintendent general

45. 「健太郎君のパパは、おまわりさんだ」と小学校2年生の次男
が言っていますが、本当はあの子のお父さんは、警視長なん
ですよ。

*"Kentarō-kun no papa wa, **omawari-san** da" to shōgakkō–ninen-
sei no jinan ga itte imasu ga, hontō wa ano ko no otōsan wa,
keishi-chō nan desu yo.*

Our second son, a second year primary schoolboy, says that "Ken-

46. 警察は半年前に北海道旅行中に行方不明*になった銀行員早瀬
    光子さんについて、捜査†を行っているそうです。

Keisatsu wa hantoshi-mae ni hokkaidō–ryokō-chū ni yukue-fumei
ni natta ginkō-in hayase mitsuko-san ni tsuite sōsa o okonatte
iru sō desu.

The police are reportedly conducting an investigation concerning
Mitsuko Hayase, a bank employee who disappeared on a trip to
Hokkaido a half year ago.

* *yukue-fumei*: become a missing person
† *sōsa*: investigation

To end on a more positive note, we might consider some of
the rights (権利 *kenri*) secured by the postwar constitution to all
persons charged with criminal offenses:

迅速な裁判を受ける権利 (*jinsoku na saiban o ukeru kenri*)
    the right to a speedy trial

弁護人を依頼する権利 (*bengo-nin o irai suru kenri*) the right
    to counsel

公開裁判の権利 (*kōkai-saiban no kenri*) the right to a public
    trial

黙秘権 (*mokuhi-ken*) the right to remain silent

一事不再理 (*ichiji–fu-sairi*) protection against repeated prose-
    cution

The difference between 一事不再理 *ichiji–fu-sairi* and the
Anglo-Saxon concept of double jeopardy is that in Japan the
prosecution is allowed to retry a defendant in the higher courts
on the basis of judicial error.

47. どんな残酷な犯罪で訴えられた人でも、弁護人を依頼する権利
    があることを忘れてはなりません。

*Donna zankoku na hanzai de uttaerareta hito de mo, **bengo-nin o
irai suru kenri** ga aru koto o wasurete wa narimasen.*

We must not forget that no matter how heinous the crime with
which one is charged, everyone has the right to counsel.

Chapter
VII

Business and Economics

In the Li Chi (礼記, J. *raiki*) or *Record of Rituals*, the last of the Chinese Five Classics (second Century B.C.), we find the following: 先財而後礼則民利. Rendered into Japanese and English, this becomes:

財を先にし礼を後にすれば民利る。
Zai o saki ni shi rei o nochi ni sureba tami musaboru.
When (the ruler) places wealth above virtue, his subjects will likewise grow greedy.

Whether this admonition has any relevance to contemporary Japan, there is clearly no doubt about the importance of 財 *zai* "money, wealth, assets, finance" as one of several word elements crucial to the world of Japanese business and economics.

財政 (*zaisei*) public finance, economy (cf. Ch. 3)
財力 (*zairyoku*) financial resources
財務 (*zaimu*) financial affairs
財界 (*zaikai*) business/financial world
財産 (*zaisan*) property, estate
財貨 (*zaika*) money and property, commodities
財団 (*zaidan*) foundation, endowment
財源 (*zaigen*) financial resources
財閥 (*zaibatsu*) financial combine/clique, zaibatsu

理財 (*rizai*) economy, finance
管財 (*kanzai*) administration of assets
私財 (*shizai*) private funds
家財 (*kazai*) household belongings
資本財 (*shihon-zai*) capital goods

Of the two readings for the character, *zai* and *sai*, the first is by far the more common. In fact, the only major exception is 財布 *saifu* "purse, wallet."

1. オニール先生によると、アメリカの最も大きな問題は赤字*財政ではなくて、家族制度が崩壊して†しまったことだそうです。

Onīru-sensei ni yoru to, amerika no mottomo ōkina mondai wa akaji-zaisei de wa nakute, kazoku-seido ga hōkai shite shimatta koto da sō desu.

According to Professor O'Neill, America's biggest problem is not her deficit finances but rather the breakdown of the family system.

 ＊ *akaji*: deficit
 † *hōkai suru*: to collapse, disintegrate

2. 日本の大蔵大臣とアメリカの財務長官の円高に関する意見が一致していないことは当然でしょう。

Nihon no ōkura-daijin to amerika no zaimu-chōkan no endaka ni kansuru iken ga itchi shite inai koto wa tōzen deshō.

It would seem only natural that the Japanese Finance Minister and the American Secretary of the Treasury would have different views regarding the appreciation of the yen.

3. 「お父さん、私に財産の分け前*をください。」

"Otōsan, watashi ni zaisan no wakemae o kudasai."

"Father, give me the portion of the property that is to be mine." (Luke 15:12, The Prodigal Son)

 ＊ *wakemae*: share, portion

4. 戦前の財閥は、まだ完全に解体された*とは言えません。

Senzen no zaibatsu wa, mada kanzen ni kaitai sareta to wa iemasen.

It cannot be said that the financial combines of the prewar period have been entirely liquidated.

 ＊ *kaitai suru*: dismantle, dissolve

5. 太平洋戦争中、収容所*に連れていかれたアメリカ西海岸の日系人のために、アルフレッド・ナガタニ氏が私財を投じて†建てようとしている博物館は、やっと実現♦のめど♠がたちました。

Taiheiyō-sensō–chū, shūyō-jo ni tsurete ikareta amerika nishi-kaigan no nikkei-jin no tame ni, arufureddo-nagatani–shi ga shizai o tōjite tateyō to shite iru hakubutsu-kan wa, yatto jitsu-gen no medo ga tachimashita.

Alfred Nagatani, who has invested his own money in an effort to build a museum for West Coast Japanese-Americans sent to internment camps during the Pacific War, is on the verge of realizing his dream.

 ＊ *shūyō-jo*: a concentration (internment) camp
 † *tōjiru*: throw, cast, invest
 ♦ *jitsugen*: materialization, realization
 ♠ *medo*: aim, goal; *medo ga tatsu* = goal comes into sight

As the semantic element in 財 (貝 shellfish, money) suggests, the meaning of the first character in 財産 *zaisan* may be understood as "financial assets." The second character, which contains the "life/birth" radical (生), may be glossed as "property," though in other contexts it means "production." No less than 財, it is a common element in words related to business.

資産 (*shisan*) property, assets

遺産 (*isan*) inheritance

不動産 (*fudōsan*) immovable property, real estate

動産 (*dōsan*) movable property

有産階級 (*yūsan-kaikyū*) bourgeosie, propertied classes (cf. Ch. 3)

無産階級 (*musan-kaikyū*) proletariat

共産 (*kyōsan*) common property, Communist

The more active sense of the word is illustrated in the following:

生産 (*seisan*) production

    生産力(性) (*seisan-ryoku/-sei*) productivity

産業 (*sangyō*) industry

    産軍複合体 (*sangun–fukugō-tai*) military-industrial complex

    産官複合体 (*sankan–fukugō-tai*) government-industrial complex

産物 (*sanbutsu*) product

    農産物 (*nō-sanbutsu*) agricultural products

    水産物 (*sui-sanbutsu*) aquatic products

    海産物 (*kai-sanbutsu*) marine products

    林産物 (*rin-sanbutsu*) forest products

    鉱産物 (*kō-sanbutsu*) mineral products

産出 (*sanshutsu*) output

産額 (*sangaku*) amount of production

産油(国) (*san'yu[-koku]*) oil producing (countries)

米産 (*beisan*) rice production

畜産 (*chikusan*) animal husbandry

国産 (*kokusan*) Japanese-made

外国産 (*gaikoku-san*) foreign-made

6. バブルがはじけた後、ほとんどの不動産は資産価値を大きく下げました。

*Baburu ga hajiketa ato, hotondo no **fudōsan** wa shisan-kachi o ōkiku sagemashita.*

Since the bubble burst, property values have fallen enormously.

7. 日本とドイツを比較すれば、労働生産性が高いのはやはりドイツですね。

*Nihon to doitsu o hikaku-sureba, rōdō–**seisan-sei** ga takai no wa yahari doitsu desu ne.*

In a comparison between Japan and Germany, it is Germany that is still higher in labor productivity.

8. 鶴子さんは、南フランスのワイン生産地に住んだことがありますが、ワインについてはよく知らないようです。

*Tsuruko-san wa, minami-furansu no wain–**seisan**-chi ni sunda koto ga arimasu ga, wain ni tsuite wa yoku shiranai yō desu.*

Although Tsuruko has lived in the wine-producing region of southern France, she does not seem to know very much about wine.

9. 日本語では「国民総生産」と言いますが、「GNP」も通じます。

*Nihongo de wa "kokumin–sō-**seisan**" to iimasu ga, "GNP" mo tsūji-masu.*

The Japanese term *kokumin–sō-seisan* [gross national product] is used [when speaking in Japanese], but "GNP" is also understood.

10. アメリカからの農産物の輸入を完全に自由化しても、国際収支*は黒字†が続くだろう。

*Amerika kara no **nō-sanbutsu** no yunyū o kanzen ni jiyū-ka shite mo, kokusai-shūshi wa kuroji ga tsuzuku darō.*

Even if imports of American agricultural products were totally liberalized, the Japan-US trade surplus would probably continue.

* *kokusai-shūshi*: balance of payment
† *kokuji*: surplus

11. 私はイギリスの産業革命以前の家庭生活に深い興味を持っています。

*Watashi wa igirisu no **sangyō**-kakumei-izen no katei-seikatsu ni fukai kyōmi o motte imasu.*

I have deep interest in English family life as it was before the industrial revolution.

12. 冷戦が終ることを予想して、ハミルトン博士は防衛産業から航空機産業に力を入れることを主張しています。

*Reisen ga owaru koto o yosō shite, hamiruton-hakase wa bōei-**sangyō** kara kōkū-ki-**sangyō** ni chikara o ireru koto o shuchō shite imasu.*

Sensing the end of the Cold War, Dr. Hamilton has been pushing for a shift in emphasis from the defense to the aircraft industry.

The second element in 産業 *sangyō* also has a wide range of meaning: "business, trade, enterprise."

「しかし、あんたはいつだって抜目のない事業家だった、ジェイ
　コブ。
事業だって……、人の道がわたしの事業だったのだ。公共の福利
　が私の事業だった。慈善が、慈悲が、寛容が、博愛が、どれも
　わたしの事業だった。」

*"Shikashi, anta wa itsu datte nukeme no nai **jigyō-ka** datta, jeikobu…"*

*"**Jigyō** datte…, hito no michi ga watashi no **jigyō** datta no da. Kōkyō no fukuri ga watashi no **jigyō** datta. Jizen ga, jihi ga, kan'yō ga, hakuai ga, doremo watashi no **jigyō** datta."*

These, in Japanese translation, are well-known words from Charles Dickens' *Christmas Carol*:

"But you were always a good man of business, Jacob…"
"Business!" cried the Ghost… "Mankind was my business; the common welfare was my business; charity, mercy, forbearance, and benevolence, were, all, my business."

Jigyō is but one of several business-related words containing 業. Here, for example, are the first four words entered under "business" in Kenkyusha's *New English-Japanese Dictionary*:

実業 (*jitsugyō*) industry, business

商業 (*shōgyō*) commerce, trade, business

職業 (*shokugyō*) occupation, business, line of work

家業 (*kagyō*) family business

業 can also appear by itself:

13. 直美は、大学でロシア文学を専攻した後翻訳を業とした。
*Naomi wa, daigaku de roshia-bungaku o senkō shita ato hon'yaku o **gyō** to shita.*

After specializing in Russian literature at her university, Naomi took up translating as a profession.

Other compounds with the character include:

業界 (*gyokai*) the business world

業務 (*gyōmu*) business (matters), work

業績 (*gyōseki*) business results

企業 (*kigyō*) enterprise, corporation

官業 (*kangyō*) government enterprise, monopoly

作業 (*sagyō*) work, operation

本業 (*hongyō*) main occupation

創業 (*sōgyō*) starting a business

営業(部) (*eigyō[-bu]*) running a business / sales department

休業 (*kyūgyō*) suspension of business operations, holiday

就業 (*shūgyō*) employment

工業 (*kōgyō*) manufacturing industry

重工業 (*jū-kōgyō*) heavy industry

軽工業 (*kei-kōgyō*) light industry

農業 (*nōgyō*) agricultural industry

漁業 (*gyogyō*) fishing industry

林業 (*ringyō*) forestry industry

繊維業 (*sen'i-gyō*) textile industry

鉱業 (*kōgyō*) mining industry

養蚕業 (*yōsan-gyō*) sericulture, silk industry

鉄鋼業 (*tekkōgyō*) steel industry

酒造業 (*shuzō-gyō*) brewing/distilling industry cf. 醸造業 *jōzō-gyō* brewing industry

製造業 (*seizō-gyō*) manufacturing industry

製鉄業 (*seitetsu-gyō*) iron industry

製紙業 (*seishi-gyō*) paper-making industry

製薬業 (*seiyaku-gyō*) pharmaceutical industry

サービス業 (*sābisu-gyō*) service industry

Read as native Japanese *waza*, 業 also means "act, deed, works, trick." The older Sino-Japanese (*go-on*) reading *gō* has a Buddhist meaning quite removed from ordinary commerce: "karma." Thus, whereas 宿屋業 *yadoya-gyō* refers to the hotel business, 宿業 *shukugō* refers to one's fate, as influenced by the consequences of a previous existence.

14. 妹は、アメリカの有名なビジネス・スクールの修士課程を終えてから、初めて実業界に向いていないことに気がつきました。

*Imōto wa, amerika no yūmei na bijinesu-sukūru no shūshi-katei o oete kara, hajimete **jitsugyō**-kai ni muite inai koto ni ki ga tsukimashita.*

My younger sister got an MA from a famous business school in America and realized only then that the business world was not for her.

15. 大阪は、昔から商業都市として知られています。

*Ōsaka wa, mukashi kara **shōgyō**-toshi to shite shirarete imasu.*

Osaka has long been known as a commercial city.

16. 小学校しか出なかった田辺さんがこんなに立派な企業家になる
とは誰も思わなかったでしょう。

*Shōgakko shika denakatta tanabe-san ga konna ni rippa na **kigyō**-ka ni naru to wa dare mo omowanakatta deshō.*

Who would have thought that Mr. Tanabe, a mere primary school graduate, would wind up such a captain of industry?

17. オーデンハイマー教授が日本の鉄鋼業の起源や発展について書
いた本は、日本語にも訳されているそうです。

*Ōdenhaimā-kyōju ga nihon no **tekkō-gyō** no kigen ya hatten ni tsuite kaita hon wa, nihon-go ni mo yakusarete iru sō desu.*

It seems that Professor Odenheimer's book on the origins and development of Japan's steel industry has even been translated into Japanese.

18. クリントン政権は、アメリカの製薬業界を攻撃していますが、
そのような非難は事実よりイデオロギーに基づいていると思い
ます。

*Kurinton-seiken wa, amerika no **seiyaku-gyōkai** o kōgeki shite imasu ga, sono yō na hinan wa jijitsu yori ideorogī ni moto-zuite iru to omoimasu.*

The Clinton administration is blasting the American pharmaceutical industry, but I think such attacks are based more on ideology than on facts.

商売 *shōbai* (lit. commerce-sale), yet another word for "trade, business," contains two more important word elements. "The dealings of my trade were but a drop of water in the comprehensive ocean of my business!" says Marley's ghost to Scrooge. The Japanese translation reads:「商売上の取引なんぞは、広大無辺の大海ともいうべき事業の一滴の水にすぎなかったのだ。」
*"**Shōbai**-jō no torihiki nanzo wa, kōdai-muhen no taikai to mo iu beki jigyō no itteki no mizu ni suginakatta no da."* Compounds with 商 *shō* include 商業 *shōgyō* "commerce," illustrated above, as well as the following:

商社 (*shōsha*) trading company

商務 (*shōmu*) commercial affairs

商品 (*shōhin*) merchandise

商店 (*shōten*) shop, store

商店街 (*shōten-gai*) shopping area

商法 (*shōhō*) way of doing business / commercial law (cf. Ch. 6)

商人 (*shōnin*) merchant

通商 (*tsūshō*) commerce, trade

通商産業省 (*tsūshō–sangyō-shō*) Ministry of International Trade and Industry (MITI = *tsūsan-shō*)

卸商 (*oroshishō*) wholesaler

小売商 (*kouri-shō*) retailer

美術商 (*bijutsu-shō*) art dealer

19. ロシア語を専攻した山田さんは、大学を卒業してから商社に入って、2年後にはモスクワに派遣されました。

*Roshia-go o senkō shita yamada-san wa, daigaku o sotsugyō shite kara **shōsha** ni haitte, ni-nen-go ni wa mosukuwa ni haken sare-mashita.*

Mr. Yamada, a Russian major, entered a trading company when he graduated from university and was posted to Moscow two years later.

20. 富田さんの奥さんは、フランス製の下着のマルチ商法に巻き込まれて、ご主人の会社にいろいろ迷惑をかけてしまいました。

*Tomita-san no okusan wa, furansu-sei no shitagi no maruchi-**shōhō** ni makikomarete, go-shujin no kaisha ni iroiro meiwaku o kakete shimaimashita.*

Mr. Tomita's wife got involved in a pyramid scheme to sell French underwear and wound up causing her husband's company a lot of trouble.

21. 金田先生は、カナダの商法の専門家です。

*Kaneda-sensei wa, kanada no **shōhō** no senmon-ka desu.*

Professor Kaneda is an expert on Canadian commercial law.

22. シェークスピアの『ベニスの商人』は、エリザベス時代のユダヤ人ぎらいを確かに反映しているかも知れませんが、それを20世紀の反ユダヤ人思想と間違えてはなりません。

*Shēkusupia no "Benisu no **shōnin**" wa, erizabesu-jidai no yudaya-jin–girai o tashika ni han'ei shite iru kamo shiremasen ga, sore wa nijusseiki no han-yudaya–shisō to machigaete wa narima-sen.*

Shakespeare's *Merchant of Venice* may very well reflect Eliza-bethan antipathy toward Jews, but such should not be confused with twentieth century anti-Semitism.

23. 家内は東洋美術を扱う美術商です。

*Kanai wa tōyō-bijutsu o atsukau **bijutsu-shō** desu.*

My wife is an art dealer dealing in East Asian art.

The native reading of 商 is *akina(u)* "trade, deal in":

24. 私はここで10年以上商いをやっています。
*Watashi wa koko de jū-nen ijō **akinai** o yatte imasu.*
I have been doing business here for over ten years.

The (somewhat archaic) native word corresponding to 商人 *shōnin* "merchant" is likewise written 商人, but the pronunciation is *akindo*, a contraction of *akibito* (*akinau hito*). Whether an *akindo* of yore or a modern 商社マン *shōsha-man* "trading company employee," those engaged in the world of commerce are ever dependent on (the state of) the economy or 経済(状態) *keizai(-jōtai)*. Here are only some of the many compounds in which this key term appears:

経済界 (*keizai-kai*) economic world/circles
経済人 (*keizai-jin*) *homo oeconomicus*
経済大国 (*keizai-taikoku*) economic giant
経済法則 (*keizai-hōsoku*) economic law/principle
経済体制 (*keizai-taisei*) economic system
経済成長 (*keizai-seichō*) economic growth
経済力 (*keizai-ryoku*) economic strength
経済政策 (*keizai-seisaku*) economic policy
経済機構 (*keizai-kikō*) economic structure
経済保証 (*keizai-hoshō*) economic security
経済危機 (*keizai-kiki*) economic crisis
経済恐慌 (*keizai-kyōkō*) economic panic
経済戦(争) (*keizai-sen[sō]*) economic warfare

25. 「経済大国日本」という極り文句をいくら聞かされても、自分の生活水準がそれほど高くはないと感じている日本人が多いだろう。
*"**Keizai-taikoku** Nippon" to iu kimari-monku o ikura kikasarete mo, jibun no seikatsu-suijun ga sore hodo takaku wa nai to kanjite iru nihon-jin ga ōi darō.*
No matter how often they may hear the cliche "Japan, economic giant," many Japanese must feel that their own standard of living is not very high.

26. 万智子さんのお父さんは、日本の経済界の有力者でした。
*Machiko-san no otōsan wa, Nihon no **keizai-kai** no yūryoku-sha deshita.*

Machiko's father was a powerful figure in Japanese economic circles.

27. 毛沢東の死去以来、中国は政治思想より経済成長を強調してい
ます。

*Mō-taku-tō no shikyo irai, chūgoku wa seiji-shisō yori **keizai-
seichō** o kyōchō shite imasu.*

Ever since the death of Mao Zedong, China has been putting economic growth ahead of political ideology.

Those who remember learning from introductory courses in
the "dismal science" (lit. 陰気な学問 *inki na gakumon*) that
"economy" derives from Greek *oikonomia* "household management" may well wonder how the combination of 経 "longitude,
warp; pass through, govern" and 済 "end, settle" can yield the
Sino-Japanese term for the same. In fact, 経済 *keizai* is originally a contracted form of 経世済民 *keisei-saimin*, lit. "govern
the world [nation], save the people."

As an advocate of laissez-faire (自由放任主義 *jiyū–hōnin-
shugi*), Adam Smith, author of *The Wealth of Nations* (「富国論」
fukoku-ron) and founder of classical economics (古典経済学
koten–keizai-gaku), might have thought that the idea smacks of
"controlled economy" (統制経済 *tōsei-keizai*). One can only
wonder what he might have thought of the following:

計画経済 (*keikaku-keizai*) planned economy

ブロック経済 (*burokku-keizai*) bloc economy

経済官僚 (*keizai-kanryō*) economic bureaucrat

保護貿易主義 (*hogo–bōeki-shugi*) protectionism

輸出奨励金 (*yushutsu–shōrei-kin*) export subsidy

関税障壁 (*kanzei-shōheki*) tariff barrier

非関税障壁 (*hi-kanzei–shōheki*) non-tariff barrier

輸入割当制 (*yunyū–wariate-sei*) import quota system

輸出の自主規制 (*yushutsu no jishu-kisei*) voluntary export quotas

28. J.K. ガルブレイス氏は、社会主義者であるかどうかわかりませ
んが、確かに計画経済の必要性を主張しています。

*J. K. garubureisu-shi wa, shakai-shugisha de aru ka dō ka wakari-
masen ga, tashìka ni **keikaku-keizai** no hitsuyō-sei o shuchō
shite imasu.*

I don't know whether John Kenneth Galbraith is a socialist or not,
but he certainly insists on the necessity of a planned economy.

29. 非関税障壁も含めて全ての貿易保護主義の手段を廃止すべきで
す。

*Hi-kanzei–shōheki mo fukumete subete no **hogo–bōeki-shugi** no shudan o haishi subeki desu.*

We should eliminate trade protection in all its forms, including non-tariff barriers.

30. アメリカの要求に応じて、日本の自動車産業は輸出の自主規制をしています。

*Amerika no yōkyū ni ōjite, nihon no jidō-sha–sangyō wa **yushutsu no jishu-kisei** o shite imasu.*

In response to American demands, the Japanese automobile industry has accepted voluntary export quotas.

No discussion of matters related to mammon would be complete without mention of 金 "gold, metal, money," whose many compounds relevant to our subject include the following:

金本位 *(kin-hon'i)* gold standard

金建て *(kindate)* the gold basis, quotations in gold

金輸出 *(kin-yushutsu)* gold export

金銭 *(kinsen)* money, cash

金額 *(kingaku)* amount of money

金利 *(kinri)* interest

金権 *(kinken)* power of money

金権政治 *(kinken-seiji)* money politics

金策 *(kinsaku)* raising money

金融 *(kin'yū)* circulation of money, money market

The last example here, 金融 (lit. "gold melting / liquidation"), is itself a phrase-formant:

金融界 *(kin'yū-kai)* the financial world

金融機関 *(kin'yū-kikan)* financial institution

金融組織 *(kin'yū-soshiki)* banking system

金融政策 *(kin'yū-seisaku)* financial policy

金融資本 *(kin'yū-shihon)* financial capital

金融緩和 *(kin'yū-kanwa)* easy money

金融引締め *(kin'yū-hikishime)* tight money

31. エイズ撲滅*のキャンペーンではかなりの金額が集まったと思います。

Eizu-bokumetsu no kyanpēn de wa kanari no kingaku ga atsumatta to omoimasu.

I think a lot of money was collected in the campaign to eradicate AIDS.

❋ *bokumetsu*: destruction, stamping out

32. あの政治家は、日本の「金権政治」をいつも非難しているのに、自分の政治資金はどこから来るのかしら。

*Ano seiji-ka wa, nihon no "**kinken-seiji**" o itsumo hinan shite iru no ni, jibun no seiji-shikin wa doko kara kuru no kashira.*

That politician is constantly denouncing Japanese "money politics," but I wonder where he gets his own political funding.

資金 *shikin* "funds, capital" is one of many examples of 金 in noninitial position:

大金 (*taikin*) an enormous sum of money

現金 (*genkin*) cash

預金 (*yokin*) bank deposit

入金 (*nyūkin*) payment, deposit

貯金 (*chokin*) savings

借金 (*shakkin*) debt

献金 (*kenkin*) contribution

頭金 (*atama-kin*) down payment

敷金 (*shikikin*) deposit (e.g., for rent)

礼金 (*reikin*) honorarium, esp. as moving-in money to a land-lord

年金 (*nenkin*) annuity, pension

賃金 (*chingin*) wages (note the shift from *k* to *g*)

33. 私たちが損したのは大金ではないけど、やはり悔しいわよ。

*Watashi-tachi ga son shita no wa **taikin** de wa nai kedo, yahari kuyashii wa yo.*

Even though the money we lost was no great fortune, it hurts just the same.

34. クレジットカードを使う日本人が最近増えましたが、普通の支払いではまだ現金です。

*Kurejitto-kādo o tsukau nihon-jin ga saikin fuemashita ga, futsū no shiharai de wa mada **genkin** desu.*

The number of Japanese using credit cards has increased recently, but the usual means of payment is still cash.

35. 昨日銀行からお金を引き出そうと思ったのに、キャッシュカードも預金通帳も見つからなくて困りました。

*Kinō ginkō kara okane o hikidasō to omotta no ni, kyasshu-kādo mo **yokin**-tsūchō mo mitsukaranakute komarimashita.*

Yesterday I wanted to go to the bank and withdraw some money, but I couldn't find either my cash card or my deposit book.

36. 借金している礼子さんたちが、あんな立派な家の頭金をどうやって手に入れたのかしら。

*Shakkin shite iru reiko-san-tachi ga, anna rippa na ie no **atama-kin** o dō yatte te ni ireta no kashira.*

Considering the debts that Reiko and her family have, I wonder how they got hold of the money for the down payment on such a splendid house.

37. いくら日本の習慣だと言っても、このような兎小屋のために6ヵ月分の「礼金」を払うなんて、どうしても不当だと思います。

*Ikura nihon no shūkan da to itte mo, kono yō na usagi-goya no tame ni rokka-getsu-bun no "**reikin**" o harau nante, dōshite mo futō da to omoimasu.*

No matter how much they say that it's a Japanese custom, I think the idea of paying six months "courtesy money" to the landlord for such a rabbit hutch is outrageous.

38. 最低賃金を引き上げることは、インフレだけではなく少数民族の失業率を高める原因にもなります。

*Saitei-**chingin** o hikiageru koto wa, infure dake de wa naku shōsū-minzoku no shitsugyō-ritsu o takameru gen'in ni mo narimasu.*

Raising the minimum wage not only causes inflation but also raises the rate of unemployment among minorities.

The words for compensation with which most readers of this book will be familiar are likely to end in 給 *kyū* "supply," read 給う *tamau* "give, grant" in native Japanese.

給与 (*kyūyo*) allowance, wages
給料 (*kyūryō*) pay
日給 (*nikkyū*) daily wages
週給 (*shūkyū*) weekly pay
月給 (*gekkyū*) monthly salary
年給 (*nenkyū*) annual salary
恩給 (*onkyū*) (civil service) pension
高給 (*kōkyū*) high salary
無給 (*mukyū*) unpaid
有給 (*yūkyū*) paid
有給休暇 (*yūkyū-kyūka*) paid holiday

39. 五十嵐君の給料はかなり低いかも知れないが、奥さんも働いているから一家の総収入*は悪くはないだろう。

*Igarashi-kun no **kyūryō** wa kanari hikui kamo shirenai ga, okusan* *mo hataraite iru kara ikka no sō-shūnyū wa waruku wa nai darō.*

Igarashi's pay may be rather low, but as his wife is also working, their combined gross income is probably not all that bad.

＊ *sō-shūnyū*: gross income

40. 25年間東大でマルクス主義経済学を教えていた高倉先生は、去年定年になった時、月に30万円の恩給をもらうことになったそうです。

*Nijūgo-nenkan tōdai de marukusu-shugi–keizai-gaku o oshiete ita takakura-sensei wa, kyonen teinen ni natta toki, tsuki ni sanjū-man-en no **onkyū** o morau koto ni natta sō desu.*

When Professor Takakura retired last year after teaching Marxist economics at the University of Tokyo for twenty-five years, he reportedly received a (civil service) pension of ¥300,000 a month.

41. 私は日給月給なので休めばそれだけ収入＊は減るのです。

*Watashi wa **nikkyū-gekkyū** na no de yasumeba sore dake shūnyū wa heru no desu.*

My monthly salary is calculated on a day-to-day basis, so the more time I take off, the less money I get.

＊ *shūnyū*: income, earnings

Native Japanese verbs for "earn" and "reward" are 稼ぐ *ka-segu* and 報いる *mukuiru*, respectively. 出稼ぎする *de-kasegi suru* refers to the act of leaving one's home in the countryside to work in a metropolis. 「徳行は自ら報ゆ」 *"tokkō wa mizukara mukuyu"* is, in classical or literary form, the Japanese counterpart of "Virtue is its own reward."

「罪の報いは死なり」 *"Tsumi no mukui wa shi nari"* says St. Paul: "The recompense of sin is death." The Greek word he uses (*opsonia*) refers originally to soldiers' 配給 *haikyū* "rations."

A similarly grim, albeit more secular, message today might be: 稼ぎの報いは税金なり *kasegi no mukui wa zeikin nari* "The recompense for earnings is taxes." As we neglected to mention this further example of a compound containing 金 in the list above, we hasten to remedy the omission with detailed examples, for unless you are a god-like politician, taxes, like death, are as inevitable in Japan as anywhere else.

The character 税 *zei* contains the "grain" radical, a reminder that the first form of taxation was agricultural. The many words it helps to form include the following:

税制 (*zeisei*) tax system
税法 (*zeihō*) method of taxation / tax law
税収 (*zeishū*) tax revenue
税率 (*zeiritsu*) tax rate
税務 (*zeimu*) tax affairs
　税務署 (*zeimu-sho*) tax office
税関 (*zeikan*) customs

課税 (*kazei*) liable for taxes
無税 (*muzei*) tax-exempt
免税(品) (*menzei[-hin]*) duty-free (goods)
関税 (*kanzei*) customs duty
納税 (*nōzei*) payment of taxes
減税 (*genzei*) tax reduction
脱税 (*datsuzei*) tax evasion

所得税 (*shotoku-zei*) income tax
国税 (*kokuzei*) national taxes
地方税 (*chihō-zei*) local taxes
住民税 (*jūmin-zei*) resident taxes
都民税 (*tomin-zei*) metropolitan taxes
区民税 (*kumin-zei*) ward taxes
市民税 (*shimin-zei*) city taxes
固定資産税 (*kotei–shisan-zei*) real estate tax
自動車税 (*jidōsha-zei*) automobile tax

相続税 (*sōzoku-zei*) inheritance tax
法人税 (*hōjin-zei*) corporate tax
物品税 (*buppin-zei*) excise tax
消費税 (*shōhi-zei*) consumer tax

累進税法 (*ruishin-zeihō*) progressive tax system
定額税法 (*teigaku-zeihō*) flat tax system
付加価値税 (*fuka-kachi–zei*) value-added tax (VAT)
源泉所得税 (*gensen–shotoku-zei*) taxation at the source, withholding taxes
源泉徴収額 (*gensen–choshū-gaku*) amount of tax withheld
源泉徴収税率 (*gensen–chōshū-zeiritsu*) rate of tax withheld

42. 収入が高ければ高いほど税率も高くなるという制度は、累進税法と呼ばれている。

法と呼ばれている。

*Shūnyū ga takakereba takai hodo **zeiritsu** mo takaku naru to iu seido wa, **ruishin–zei–hō** to yobarete iru.*

The system whereby tax rates rise as income rises is called progressive taxation.

43. 定額税法は今の税制より確かに簡単で、最終的には公平でもあると思います。

Teigaku-zeihō wa ima no zeisei yori tashika ni kantan de, saishū-teki ni wa kōhei de mo aru to omoimasu.

A flat-tax system is certainly simpler than the present system, and I believe it is also ultimately fairer.

44. 留美子さんは、来月から空港の免税店で働くことになりました。

*Rumiko-san wa, raigetsu kara kūkō no **menzei**-ten de hataraku koto ni narimashita.*

Rumiko is going to be working in the airport duty-free shop beginning next month.

45. 去年アメリカから持って来たコンピュータには関税がかからなかった。

*Kyonen amerika kara motte kita konpyūta ni wa **kanzei** ga kakara-nakatta.*

I didn't have to pay any customs duty on the computer I brought from America last year.

46. 国税はきちんと払っていても、区民税や市民税を払ったことのない外国人が多いようです。

*Kokuzei wa kichinto haratte ite mo, **kumin-zei** ya **shimin-zei** o haratta koto no nai gaikoku-jin ga ōi yō desu.*

There appear to be many foreigners who pay national taxes as they should but who have never paid ward taxes or metropolitan taxes.

47. 野田さんは相続税を払うためにあの藁葺き*屋根の家を売ってしまいました。

*Noda-san wa **sōzoku-zei** o harau tame ni ano warabuki-yane no ie o utte shimaimashita.*

Mr. Noda wound up selling that straw-thatched roof house in order to pay inheritance taxes.

＊ *warabuki*: thatched with straw

48. 消費税が導入された*時の強い反対は、何時の間にか消えてしまいました。

Shōhi-zei ga dōnyū sareta toki no tsuyoi hantai wa, itsu no ma ni ka kiete shimaimashita.

The strong opposition with which the consumer tax was met when it was first introduced faded away all too soon.

49. 日本の源泉徴収率は、欧米の諸国と比較すれば一般に低い。

*Nihon no **gensen–chōshū-ritsu** wa, ōbei no shokoku to hikaku sure-ba ippan ni hikui.*

The rate at which taxes are withheld in Japan is generally lower than in Europe and America.

On that happy note, we turn finally to various means to let one's assets grow, ranging from savings accounts to the stock market. Here first are a few essential terms for getting around at one's neighborhood bank or post office:

銀行預金口座 (*ginkō–yokin-kōza*) bank account

定期預金 (*teiki-yokin*) fixed deposit, time deposit

普通預金 (*futsū-yokin*) ordinary account

当座預金 (*tōza-yokin*) checking account

預金金利 (*yokin-kinri*) interest rate on savings account

預金残高 (*yokin-zandaka*) bank balance

振込み (*furikomi*) bank transfer

手数料 (*tesū-ryō*) handling fee

貸し金 (*kashikin*) loan, cf. 貸し出し *kashidashi*, ローン *rōn* "loan"

貸出金利 (*kashidashi-kinri*) loan rate

住宅ローン (*jūtaku-rōn*) housing loan

外国為替 (*gaikoku-kawase*) foreign exchange

送金 (*sōkin*) (lit. send-money) remittance (+ *suru*)

郵便貯金 (*yūbin-chokin*) postal savings

自動支払機 (*jidō–shiharai-ki*) automatic teller machine

50. 恵津子さんのけちなご主人は、宝くじで一等が当たった時、そのお金をすぐ自分の定期預金にして彼女に一銭も使わせなかった。

*Etsuko-san no kechi na go-shujin wa, takara-kuji de ittō ga atatta toki, sono okane o sugu jibun no **teiki-yokin** ni shite kanojo ni issen mo tsukawasenakatta.*

When Etsuko's tight-fisted husband won first prize in the lottery, he promptly put the money in his own time deposit account and wouldn't let her touch a penny of it.

51. スポーツクラブの会員費は銀行振込みで支払っているので、いくらなのか正確には覚えていません。

*Supōtsu-kurabu no kai'in-hi wa **ginkō-furikomi** de shiharatte iru no de, ikura na no ka seikaku ni wa oboete imasen.*

As I pay the sports club membership fee by bank transfer, I don't remember the exact amount.

52. 先週の円・ドル為替レート*がよかったから、弟に400ドル送金
しようと思ったけれど、手数料が高いことが分かったので、ア
メリカの当座預金を使って小切手を送ることにしました。

*Senshū no en-doru kawase-rēto ga yokatta kara, otōto ni yon-hyaku-doru **sōkin** shiyō to omotta keredo, **tesū-ryō** ga takai koto ga wakatta no de, amerika no **tōza-yokin** o tsukatte kogitte o okuru koto ni shimashita.*

Since last week's yen-dollar exchange rate was favorable, I wanted to wire $400 to my younger brother, but when I realized how high the commission was, I decided to send him a check instead, using my American checking account.

＊ kawase-rēto: exchange rate

53. 自動支払機を使う人が多いから、時々故障するのは仕方があり
ません。

Jidō–shiharai-ki *o tsukau hito ga ōi kara, tokidoki koshō suru no wa shikata ga arimasen.*

Since the automatic teller machines are used by so many people, I suppose it is only to be expected that they will break down once in a while.

What British English speakers call "shares" and American English speakers "stocks" goes by the name of 株 *kabu* (lit. stump, root). Those brave or shrewd enough to dabble in the market (株に手を出す *kabu ni te o dasu*) will need to know far more than is provided here. The following are only a few basic terms:

株主 (*kabunushi*) shareholder
株式市場 (*kabushiki-shijō*) stock market
株取引き (*kabu-torihiki*) dealing in stock
株価 (*kabuka*) stock prices
配当 (*haitō*) dividend
東京証券取引所 (*tōkyō-shōken-torihiki-jo*) Tokyo Stock Exchange
日経ダウ平均 (*nikkei-dau–heikin*) Nikkei Dow Jones average
株式市況 (*kabushiki-shikyō*) stock market situation
株式会社 (*kabushiki-gaisha*) joint stock company
普通株 (*futsū-kabu*) ordinary stock
上場株 (*jōjō-kabu*) listed stock
非上場株 (*hi-jōjō–kabu*) unlisted stock
店頭売買株 (*tentō-baibai–kabu*) over-the-counter stock

証券 (*shōken*) securities

国債 (*kokusai*) government bond

投資 (*tōshi*) investment (+ *suru*)

54. 森田さんは、15年前に買った株が値上がりして今では配当だけ
で食べています。

*Morita-san wa, jūgo-nen mae ni katta **kabu** ga ne-agari shite ima de wa **haitō** dake de tabete imasu.*

The stock that Mr. Morita bought fifteen years ago has gone up so much that he now lives off the dividends.

55. 日経ダウ平均から見れば、先週から続いている円高は株主にと
って決して喜ばしいニュースではないでしょう。

***Nikkei-dau–heikin** kara mireba, senshū kara tsuzuite iru endaka wa **kabunushi** ni totte kesshite yorokobashii nyūsu de wa nai deshō.*

To judge from the Nikkei Dow Jones average, the rise of the yen that has continued since last week is by no means good news for share holders.

56. なぜ株も国債も買わないのかと聞かれる度に、私の祖父は何時
もシェークスピアのポローニアスと同じことを言った。「借り
手にも貸し手にもなるな。」ポローニアスは馬鹿者かもしれな
いが、祖父は賢明な事業家だった。

*Naze **kabu** mo **kokusai** mo kawanai no ka to kikareru tabi ni, watashi no sofu wa itsumo shēkusupia no porōniasu to onaji koto o itta. "Kari-te ni mo kashi-te ni mo naru na." Porōniasu wa bakamono kamo shirenai ga, sofu wa kenmei na jigyō-ka datta.*

Whenever my grandfather was asked why he bought neither company shares nor government bonds, he always used the words of Shakespeare's Polonius: "Neither a borrower nor a lender be." I suppose Polonius was a fool, but Grandfather was a wise man of business.